DYSLEXIA AND SPELLING

by the same author

Dyslexia Advocate!
How to Advocate for a Child with Dyslexia within the Public Education System
Kelli Sandman-Hurley
ISBN 978 1 84905 737 0
eISBN 978 1 78450 274 4

of related interest

The Big Book of Dyslexia Activities for Kids and Teens
100+ Creative, Fun, Multi-sensory and Inclusive Ideas for Successful Learning
Gavin Reid, Nick Guise and Jennie Guise
ISBN 978 1 78592 377 7
eISBN 978 1 78450 725 1

Fun Games and Activities for Children with Dyslexia
How to Learn Smarter with a Dyslexic Brain
Alais Winton
Illustrated by Joe Salerno
ISBN 978 1 78592 292 3
eISBN 978 1 78450 596 7

The Illustrated Guide to Dyslexia and Its Amazing People
Kate Power and Kathy Iwanczak Forsyth
Foreword by Richard Rogers
ISBN 978 1 78592 330 2
eISBN 978 1 78450 647 6

Dyslexia is My Superpower (Most of the Time)
Margaret Rooke
Forewords by Professor Catherine Drennan and Loyle Carner
ISBN 978 1 78592 299 2
eISBN 978 1 78450 606 3

DYSLEXIA AND SPELLING

Making Sense of It All

Kelli Sandman-Hurley

Jessica Kingsley *Publishers*
London and Philadelphia

First published in 2019
by Jessica Kingsley Publishers
73 Collier Street
London N1 9BE, UK
and
400 Market Street, Suite 400
Philadelphia, PA 19106, USA

www.jkp.com

Library of Congress Cataloging in Publication Data
A CIP catalog record for this book is available from the Library of Congress

British Library Cataloguing in Publication Data
A CIP catalogue record for this book is available from the British Library

ISBN 978 1 78592 791 1
eISBN 978 1 78450 760 2

Printed and bound by CPI Group (UK) Ltd, Croydon, CR0 4YY

To Rick and Casey, I am so grateful for our little family and your unconditional love. I am lucky to have you both.

To the great people who took the time to read this book and offer feedback, specifically Tracy, Pete, Sue and Dad. I am eternally grateful!

To my dad, who has been my editor with the most honest feedback since...always.

To my mom, for always being proud of me.

Dyslexia is Real.

Spelling Matters.

#spellingrevolution

Contents

Preface

I began my career in literacy working at the adult literacy program of the San Diego Public Library. During my time there I met hundreds of adults with low literacy skills who often cried when they spoke about their school experiences. They told stories of struggling to read to their children because of their own literacy struggles. They described the obstacles they faced in getting a new and/or better job because they could not spell. I remember one student's emotional story about not being able to write a letter to his son because his spelling was so bad. Every single student I worked with included spelling as one of their literacy goals because they thought it was an important skill for their everyday lives. As I transitioned to helping younger dyslexic students and their families, I continued to seek out trainings that were based on evidence and widely accepted in the dyslexia community. I was trained and studied just about everything, but something was missing. There seemed to be so much emphasis placed on memorization techniques and lists of rules to apply. My students often asked me, "Why?" and I was left with the response, "English is just crazy, now let's get back to that sight-word study method to help you memorize this crazy word."

I never believe that I know everything I need to know about reading and spelling. In fact, the more I learn the more I realize how much I still don't know. That openness led me to a meeting at a conference that changed my professional life forever and challenged everything I had been taught in every training I had ever attended.

I was at a dyslexia conference and I noticed that there was a bit of a frenzy at a booth near me in the convention hall. My initial thought was that it was another snake-oil salesman trying to dupe the dyslexia community to make some money. But as I sat and watched, I thought, there must be something there that is legitimate because that many people in this community cannot be duped. So, I walked over to Dr. Peter Bowers and said, "Okay, so tell me what you are talking about here." He replied, "Give me one English word that you think is crazy and nonsensical." I immediately gave him the word *sign*, which he wrote down on a cocktail napkin. We had a brief discussion about what *sign* means and within one minute we were talking about the connection in meaning and spelling between *sign* and *signal*. In that one minute I felt like someone had ripped the blindfold off my eyes. I couldn't believe I had gone through years and years of education about education and training after training about teaching English to struggling learners and not once did someone show me what Dr. Bowers showed me in less than one minute. I was immediately disappointed in my education, but more importantly, I was hyper-motivated to find out more. This was what my students needed: to see the connections between words and understand the whys of words, and be shown how to figure this out on their own, independently, like the curious, thoughtful individuals that they are.

Since that brief meeting, myself and my staff have been immersed in the studying of English orthography with others like the brilliant linguist at Real Spelling and Dr. Bowers, and the content of this book is heavily influenced and informed by their scientific (yes, linguistics is a science) work. As a professional in the dyslexia community I feel a great deal of responsibility to investigate all avenues and ideas that are presented to me; some are crazy and easy to dismiss and some are so compelling, like the lesson of *sign*, that it drives me to go back to school to understand as much as I can. It would be impossible to fit everything you should know about English to help our struggling students in a book like this, so I highly encourage you to continue your education past this book by consulting the resource section for valuable courses, blogs and instructional aids.

This book is intended to give you an introduction to why spelling is hard for students with dyslexia, and others, to help you understand and use the reading and spelling terms accurately and then offer some instructional strategies. This book is not a new program or approach, it is a resource to offer you, the professional, information that you can use to improve your students' ability to understand how the English orthography is actually structured. Hopefully, by the end of the book you will feel confident enough to get excited when you and your student/s come to words that seems illogical and then investigate your way through the word to understand it together.

Most importantly, this book is about honesty and integrity. As the mother of an elementary (primary) school student, I want him to learn the truth about English. I know he is capable. I know his friends are capable. I know that he is interested, and I know his friends are interested. The information in this book is not new or something I created, it is not a program or a method or approach, it is just the facts about the English writing system and it is up to you to figure out how to deliver this book of truths to your students. There is a glossary at the end of the book that explains any terms related to spelling and writing.

Key to markings used in this book

When writing about English spelling in an accurate way, there are notations that can be used to differentiate when we are referring to phonetic and phonemic spellings.

< >	Letters between these symbols show the spelling of the word; they are a letter string and should be spelled out, not pronounced.	<bold> + <ly>
//	Phonemic representation	table = /teɪbl/ catch = /kætʃ/
[ ]	Phonetic representation	[dɪslɛksiə]
*	This indicates an incorrect spelling	*<acshun>

> Orthography is the writing system of a language.

This is a book about helping struggling students understand English *orthography*. That understanding can shift the way we talk about the English writing system from memorization techniques and sounding-it-out strategies to discovering the reasons for spellings. This shift can improve our students' attitudes towards spelling, because if we are constantly berating English as illogical, we send the message that it is pointless to try to understand it.

> A phoneme is the smallest contrastive unit in the sound system of a language. The phonemes /b/ and /r/ distinguish the word bat from rat.

> Phonetics is the term used to describe speech sounds. This includes the articulatory features to produce speech and the sounds that are produced.

In order to begin talking about spelling with students in an accurate way, we have to begin using, and understanding, the correct terminology, and we have to understand some basic spelling patterns before we guide the discovery process. And yes, I am suggesting using the terminology listed below with kids as young as kindergarten (year 1) age. If you think I am crazy, try it first. Think about this: we talk about dinosaurs with kids of this age without a second thought, using words like tyrannosaurus and triceratops—why do we think the term *phoneme* is too hard for students?

Before you start on your journey, which I hope will be as eye-opening as mine was, consider this word:

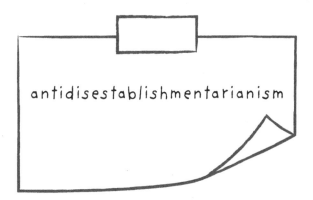

By the time you reach the end of the book you should be able to come up with at least a hypothesis about the spelling.

Lastly, the information in this book is not intended to create perfect spellers; none of us are perfect spellers. It is also not intended to be the end of your leaning, it should be just the beginning—consider it an introduction. The intention is to help you, and your students, change the questions that are asked during spelling instruction and then dig deeper. Students should begin to understand there is a reason for spellings and you should begin to understand how to help them through the process to find that reason. Remember that students with dyslexia are good problem solvers and pattern seekers, so helping them discover the logic of the English spelling system seems like a natural teaching choice. The result should be more mindful spelling; not perfect spelling, but mindful.

Why Spelling is so Hard

You can see a phone, but you cannot see a phoneme.

Linguistics Professor

Spelling. It is described as crazy and often declared unimportant. Spelling lists are created with random, unrelated words and taught via rote memorization techniques. It is taught out of context and isolated from grammar. This is a disastrous combination for kids with dyslexia and troublesome for many kids without dyslexia. Of course, many students will learn to spell without a hitch, but does that make it okay? Read on to become part of a spelling revolution.

How many times have you seen the word *does* spelled *<dose> or the word *two* as *<tow> and maybe *spelled* as *<speld>, even after the student has studied these words repeatedly? These spellings are the result of the first strategy kids are taught when learning how to spell (and read), which is to "sound it out." So, let's put this strategy to the test. Grab a pen (or pencil or keyboard with autocorrect disabled) and write the directions to making a peanut butter and jelly (jam) sandwich. Make sure to include every little detail from getting a knife out of the drawer to opening the lids on the jars. But make sure that while you are writing those directions you are sounding out every word and spelling each word exactly as it sounds. There are no right or wrong answers, spell the words as you pronounce them. Stop here until you are done. Once you have finished this task take a look at what you have written. I am willing to bet you have something like this:

Frst u nede a pece uv bred. Then git sum penut budr and a nife.

Now, this is my American English interpretation of words like *get* and *butter.* If you speak another dialect of English, you may have spelled *butter* as *<butr>; remember that there are no wrong answers. Now think about this: how fast did the sounding-it-out strategy fall apart for you? In the first sentence? Maybe even the first word? I am also willing to guess that was relatively difficult for you. Have you seen spelling like this before? Perhaps in your classroom or your child's homework? Students who spell this way are not doing anything wrong. They are doing exactly what we teach them to do— they are sounding out the words. When the sounding-it-out approach fails them they are then taught to think the word is crazy, nonsensical and just a word to be memorized. But let's think about that for a minute. A student who struggles with understanding and remembering written language is now being told to memorize written language, with no sense attached to it. Where is the sense in that?

For students with dyslexia, spelling English words cannot be reduced to either sounding it out or memorizing it. In fact, it shouldn't be reduced to this for students without dyslexia either. When they do sound it out and end up spelling words like the words you spelled while writing directions for the sandwich, they end up with a lot of red marks on their papers. They tend to begin to use smaller words that they are more confident they can spell. By doing that they produce work that is not representative of their actual intellectual ability. And by doing that they begin to feel inferior to their peers who can spell.

Students with dyslexia need to understand that the English writing system is not a random collection of words with letters included for no reason. Although, in most curriculum manuals, that is how it is presented. Words are introduced as either regular or irregular. Crazy or sane. Decodable or sight word. But this is all a huge misunderstanding by the education community. Spelling is driven by morphology (structure and meaning), etymology (history) and phonology (sound system of a particular language). Written word families have evolved through time to convey meaning first and represent phonology second, and this is demonstrated by the evolution of a word that shifts pronunciation but not spelling. Think of the word *been* and its different English pronunciations throughout the world. Even though the way most Americans pronounce that word is different than most British speakers, the spelling does not change.

Why is it so hard for kids with dyslexia to spell?

First, we have to understand what dyslexia is and what it is not. According to the International Dyslexia Association (IDA):

> Dyslexia is characterized by difficulties with accurate and/ or fluent word recognition and by *poor spelling* and decoding abilities. These difficulties typically result from a deficit in the phonological component of language that is often unexpected in relation to other cognitive abilities and the provision of effective classroom instruction. Secondary consequences may include problems in reading comprehension and reduced reading experience that can impede growth of vocabulary and background knowledge. (IDA, 2019) (This definition was adopted by the IDA Board of Directors on November 12, 2002 and is also used by the National Institute of Child Health and Human Development (NICHD).)

I took the liberty of emphasizing *poor spelling* in the IDA's definition. Spelling is highlighted because when people talk about dyslexia they often refer to reading and make no mention of spelling, and the fact is that just about everyone with dyslexia struggles with spelling (IDA, 2011). Some students with dyslexia are decent readers but poor spellers, and those students are often overlooked. This oversight is usually accompanied by a comment about spelling not being important.

Signs and symptoms of dyslexia

Before we can talk about how to teach spelling, we have to have at least a cursory understanding of what dyslexia is and is not. For a more thorough explanation of dyslexia, please see the list of dyslexia resources at the end of this book.

The following is a list of signs and symptoms of dyslexia. While you are reading through this list it is important to understand that there is not one profile for a student with dyslexia. Dyslexia occurs on a continuum and can be mild to moderate to severe to profound. One child with dyslexia might have extreme difficulty with basic reading tasks, while another may be able to decode but have difficulty with spelling, and another might have trouble with reading fluency. It is extremely important to determine the strengths and weaknesses of each individual in order to determine what is appropriate for them to improve their literacy skills (Sandman-Hurley, 2016).

- Difficulty decoding words in isolation: This is assessed by having the student read words out of context—the lists are usually filled with unrelated words. This is often more difficult for children with dyslexia because they have to rely on their limited knowledge of the structure of English words to decode isolated words without the benefit of context. Without context there is no way to know how to pronounce a word like *produce* because the context will determine where the stress is in the word and that stress placement will determine if it is a verb or a noun. For example, are you referring to the *produce* in the grocery store or are you referring to a product you are going to *produce*? Additionally, the pronunciation of some graphemes, like <ch>, depends on the etymology, which isolated lists do not provide.

- Difficulty with spelling: Children with dyslexia almost always struggle with spelling and are often relying on the sounding-it-out strategy they have been taught. For example, they might spell *spilled* as *<spild> or *<spilld>.

- Difficulty with *phonemic understanding*: For example, your student may have difficulty understanding, or articulating, that the word *cat* has three phonemes, /c/ /a/ /t/, and may instead say it the following way: /c/ /at/.

Phonemic understanding is the ability of the student to verbally manipulate the phonemes of a language.

- Difficulty with *phonological understanding*: Phonological understanding is the ability to manipulate the language sounds in a particular language, which includes identifying individual words, to word parts or syllables, and then into the smallest parts called phonemes or speech sounds.

- Slow, laborious reading: Children with dyslexia might read a passage or sentences very slowly, trying to decode (sound out) each and every word. This difficulty is more pronounced when larger, polysyllabic words are included in the text.

- Difficulty with math problems: A child with dyslexia who is struggling with reading might also struggle to read math problems.

- Reversing letters passed the second grade (year 3): The reversal of b and d, as well as other letters, is normal through the first grade (year 2); after that it becomes a red flag.

Spelling is more difficult for students with dyslexia because they have difficulty processing and storing language and that makes accessing words from memory difficult. A phonological memory weakness is common for students with dyslexia. Phonological memory measures the individual's ability to code information phonologically for temporary storage in working or short-term memory (Wagner *et al.*, 2013). Students often search for related words that are connected by meaning (Nagy *et al.*, 1989), but if they do not understand those connections this becomes difficult.

As important as it is to understand what dyslexia is, it is equally important to understand what it is not.

- Dyslexia is not caused by poor eyesight or hearing problems. Vision Therapy or Color Overlays will not help. This bullet point is sure to raise eyebrows, so I encourage you to read through the meta-analysis done by the American Academy of Pediatrics for the evidence to support this point (American Academy of Pediatrics *et al.*, 2009).

- Dyslexia is not seeing words or letters backwards. Yes, many students with dyslexia do confuse their *b*s and their *d*s, but it is not because they see the letters backwards. This confusion happens because they have difficulty learning that when certain letters change their spatial orientation they also change their phonology and grapheme status. For example, when you look at a picture of an elephant and then flip the picture over it is still an elephant. When we present students with a <b> and then change it to a <d> everything about it changes. It is normal to confuse letters through the end of the first grade (year 2), but after that it becomes a symptom of dyslexia. But it's just one small symptom and not all students with dyslexia do it.

- Dyslexia is not a developmental disability.

- Dyslexia is not acquired alexia, aphasia or anomia—these are caused by some type of head injury (e.g. stroke).

- Dyslexia is not a degenerative disease.

- Dyslexia is not lack of educational opportunity.

- Dyslexia is not the result of laziness or a lack of effort on the part of the student.

- Dyslexia not just a weakness in phonological understanding. Many students might not have a weakness in this area and might even have a phonological understanding strength but not be able to transfer that strength to the orthography. These students have difficulty remembering "sight words" (words that cannot be "sounded out," such as *sign*, *two* and *was*) and have difficulty with spelling. This is a weakness in orthographic understanding.

Many students will see a word a few times and remember how to spell it, but for those students with dyslexia who tend to have a more difficult time committing spellings to memory or who get frustrated with the inconsistent strategy of sounding out words, these students, really all students, need to understand the reasons behind the spellings. We need to remove the amount of pressure being placed on their memory to recall words instead of helping them understand spellings deeply. In order to do that, we, as teachers, need to understand it ourselves. This book is not intended to be a guide that tells you to do this first and do that second. This book was designed to give you the information you need to understand the true structure of the English language so that you can use that knowledge to create individualized lessons with your struggling students. Additionally, while this book is geared towards working with students with dyslexia, it is really imperative that every student, and teacher, has this information about their own language. Our kids deserve for us to make this improvement in our understanding. It can be uncomfortable and scary to admit that there were things about English that we didn't understand and we may have been teaching it erroneously to our students, but when you have the evidence from the language itself you cannot help but change the way you teach it.

Food for thought: Sidebar about the term *awareness*

In the education world, it is very common to use terms like phonological awareness, phonemic awareness, orthographic awareness and morphological awareness. But since this is a book about being accurate with our language, maybe we should revisit that terminology. Do we want our students to be aware or do we want them to understand? Perhaps it's time to change those terms to better reflect the outcome we want. How about: phonemic understanding, phonological understanding and morphological understanding?

Morphological understanding to improve spelling

> Morphology is the study of the internal structure of a word, which is made up of morphemes. A morpheme is the smallest meaningful unit in a word. For example, the word **plays** is two morphemes: play + s → plays.

Educational research is often studied through the lens that phonology is the primary influence on spelling, while failing to understand, or study, the primary role of morphology. Notably, Ehri (2000) developed a much-referenced developmental spelling continuum in which it is suggested that morphology should be introduced, but not until a much later stage, after children have "mastered" phonics. This ignores the fact that students in kindergarten (year 1) come to school with an understanding about spoken English morphology, which is evidenced when they verbally add a <-s> suffix to a base word to indicate the pluralized form of that word like *cats* or the third person singular verb like *runs*. They are even able to change the pronunciation of the suffix <-s> of /dagz/ and /kæts/ implicitly (Berko, 1958). Yet they go to school and learn written syllables, which does not give them the opportunity to leverage what they understand about morphology, instead it contradicts what they already implicitly understand. Again, most students will have no problem with this contradiction to what they implicitly know, but students with dyslexia can be very confused by this imbalance. A Nunes, Bryant and Bindman (1997) study supported the Ehri stage hypothesis, but with a caveat: they suggested that while it may be developmentally normal to spell phonetically [sic] before transitioning to morphological spelling, the transition is aided by "explicit grammatical awareness," which means students understand that when morphemes are added to words they can change the word from one part of speech to another. For example, adding a suffix <-s> to the base <cat> changes the word from a singular noun to a plural noun. Carlisle (2010, p.480) stated that "even kindergartners can acquire morphological awareness, if this is what they are taught," which is the crucial point—*if they are taught.*

An affix is a morpheme that is joined to a base or root. An affix can be a suffix or a prefix. In the word **replayed,** <re-> is the prefix, <play> is the base and <-ed> is the suffix.

Research aside, the fact that the current research studies spelling structure from a phonology-first perspective, without regard to the role that meaning plays in spelling, places the spelling stages into question. Does it really make sense to withhold suffixes like <-ly> and <-ion> from students when kindergarten-age kids (year 1) clearly come into contact with words like *likely* and *action*? Where is the evidence that withholding this information is better than teaching it earlier? Why do we wait so long to talk about *vowel digraphs* like the <oo> in *school*?

A vowel digraph is two graphemes (e.g. <oo>) that spell one phoneme.

Etymology is the study of the origins and
history of words.

The explicit teaching of morphological understanding in early grades is not a part of the current school curriculum, so those questions remain unanswered. In fact, Bowers, Kirby and Deacon (2010) argue that there is no evidence for waiting to teach the intersection of morphology, phonology and etymology to younger children. In fact, studies have been conducted that provide some evidence that this type of explicit instruction actually benefits the younger children as well as struggling readers and spellers (Kirby *et al.*, 2011). Leong (2000) concluded that knowledge of morphology, semantics and syntax should improve reading and spelling. His study supported an earlier finding from Shankweiler *et al.* (2009, cited in Leong, 2000) that struggling students lacked a "knowledge of derived forms and other morphological relations...awareness of English spelling conventions... knowledge of word families, all of which are held to be important for spelling" (p.289). Carlisle (2010) also noted that a student's knowledge of morphology can also lead to improved word recognition. The spelling mistakes made by young and struggling students (e.g. *<kisst> and *<vacashun>) often reveal a lack of understanding of the role morphology plays in the English spelling in words like *kissed* and *vacation*, which is a contradiction to what they understand about their spoken language.

> A grapheme is a letter, or a group of letters, that represent a phoneme. In the word **chip** there are four letters: c, h, i, p and three graphemes: ch - i - p. In the word **chips,** there are five letters: c, h, i, p, s and four graphemes: ch - i - p - s and two morphemes: chip + s.

> A base is the current spelling of an English word. Bases can be either bound or free. In the word **replayed, play** is the free base. In the word **structure, struct** is a bound base.

Kemp, Mitchell and Bryant (2017) explain that the morphological structure of the word will determine the spelling more than the pronunciation will. For example, the *affix* <-ed> changes its phonology based on the articulation of the last *grapheme* of the *base* or affix, /spɛld/, /wɛldɪd/ and /laɪkt/, or previous morpheme, but the spelling does not change. The results of the Kemp *et al.* study also supported previous research that showed that students who do not have explicit instruction in morphology do not use this information when they spell, which suggests it needs to be explicitly taught. Finally, English does offer morphological information to readers and spellers that would improve their ability to spell (Aronoff, Berg and Heyer, 2016) but that information is not introduced until much later in the learning-to-read-and-spell process. And before we go on, make no mistake—this is not a book about teaching morphology. This is a book about the intersection of morphology, etymology and phonology; it is here that we can truly understand English spellings.

Dispelling (pun intended) common myths about English
Myth #1: Morphology is for older students

Morphology research is not limited to the education world. In fact, there is a plethora of research about young children and their understanding of morphology in the linguistic research base, but that research is often not cited in educational journals. In 1958 Jeanne Berko conducted a famous experiment, called the Wug test. During this test, kindergarteners and first graders (years 1 and 2) were given the following sentence using a word that the students had not heard before: "This is a wug. Now there is another one. There are two of them. There are two _____" (Berko, 1958, p.155). The students' answers were not only correct when answering /wʌgz/, but Berko concluded that "they were consistent and orderly answers, and they demonstrated that there can be no doubt that children in this age range operate with clearly delimited morphological rules" (Berko, 1958, p.171). This was just the beginning of understanding that young children do implicitly understand the morphological rules of their language, yet we teach them something different when they get to school. In particular, students with dyslexia will experience extreme frustration when learning to spell due to this inconsistency in how English is taught.[1]

---

1   While students do continue to grow and develop in their morphological understanding in spelling throughout the elementary school years (years 2–6) (Apel, Diehm and Apel, 2013; Berninger et al., 2010), it is quite likely that we are missing an opportunity to explicitly introduce it earlier, as evidenced by Bowers, Kirby and Deacon (2010) and Goodwin and Ahn (2003).

Myth #2: The English writing system is based on syllables

This is inaccurate and the proof is easily discovered when we look to the words themselves as evidence. For example, let's look at the spelling of the word *action*. In most spelling and reading programs, this word is taught to the student as ac/tion, because if you look in most dictionaries, the word *action* can be pronounced the following way (see the glossary for an explanation of the International Phonetic Alphabet (IPA) symbols): /ækʃən/, but that pronunciation does not explain the spelling, hence our students' constant confusion and frustration with the inconsistencies of spelling and pronunciation. Now let's look at the word *action* in the way it is actually structured. The base is <act> and the suffix is <-ion>. There is no way around that fact, especially when you look at other words you build with an <act> base (there will be more on locating bases in Chapter 2), like *acting, active, deactivate*, etc. By this time, I am sure you are looking at that <-ion> and thinking, that is not a suffix, *<-tion> is the suffix—nope, not true, anywhere, on any word. If that were true, then the base would be *<ac> and that can't be because *<ac> doesn't mean anything, but <act> does. Additionally, we need the <act> base to build related words like *active, acts, reactive*, etc. These other related words and their suffixes provide us with the evidence we need to understand that the final <t> is part of the base.

This brings us to the fact that the English writing system is not built on written syllables, but instead it is *morphophonemic*. Morphophonemic means that when words are built with more than one morpheme we do not know how the word will be pronounced until we know which morphemes are added or deleted and how they will interact with each other phonologically. For example, in the word *action* the grapheme <t> is pronounced as /ʃ/ but in the word *acting* the <t> is pronounced as /t/ and in *actually* the pronunciation of <t> is /tʃ/. Below is a lexical matrix to visually represent this concept:

re	**\<act\>**	ion		
		ive		
		s		
		u	al	ly

Word sums created from this matrix:

act + s → acts

re + act + ive → reactive

re + act + ion → reaction

act + ion → action

act + ion + s → actions

act + u + al + ly → actually

act + ive → active

All lexical matrices in this book were created using a free resource at: www.neilramsden.co.uk/spelling/matrix.

Myth #3: English is crazy

Nope. It only appears that way because it is not taught accurately or even understood properly. Interestingly, almost every linguistic textbook I have ever come across describes the English language as elegant. In fact, Richard Venezky explained English spelling in the following way:

...the simple fact is that the present orthography is not merely a letter-to-sound system riddled with imperfections, but, instead, a more complex and more regular relationship wherein phoneme and morpheme share leading roles. (Venezky, 1967, p.77)

Myth #4: Spelling isn't important

Recently, I have noticed that people who say spelling isn't important while they are talking about how to teach a struggling student are usually people who can spell. After spending over 12 years working with adult literacy learners, I never heard one of them say that they didn't want to know how to spell. I once asked a group of dyslexic kids if they wanted to know how to spell and every single hand went emphatically into the air. It can be embarrassing to spell things wrong. It can hinder really good thoughts from getting to paper, even after you tell students not to worry about spelling. The fact is that this really isn't about spelling or being a perfect speller, it's about changing the conversation about spelling and understanding why words are spelled the way they are. While they are learning to spell, students may still struggle, but at least they will have different questions about spelling because they will start to see the sense of it. Instead of exclaiming that English is crazy, they will ponder and hopefully say to you, "Hmm, I wonder why there is a <g> in *sign*," because they will understand there is a reason. No more memorization strategies, just straight, logical understanding. Is there a time and place for spellcheck and voice to text? Absolutely, but not in place of building an understanding. Spelling is important; it changes how we communicate and how we think.

Syllables and morphemes: which one makes more sense?

As I have stated previously, this book is not a new program or approach, it is an informational text meant to include information that might be useful to those who are working with struggling spellers and readers.

Let's circle back to the fact that because the English writing system is not based on written syllables, it is more accurate to teach the true underlying structure of English. To illustrate this point, the chart below compares words side by side. They are divided by syllables and morphemes. What do you notice?

Word	Syllable division	Morphology
elevate	el ev ate	e + lev + ate
circular	cir cu lar	circ + ule + ar
thermometer	ther mom et er	therm + o + mete + er
motivation	mo tiv a tion	mote + ive + ate + ion
blaming	bla ming	blame + ing

When the word *elevate* is divided into syllables, the first syllable is *el*, which interrupts the base of the word, which is *lev*. The base is essential to the meaning of the word and its connection to its relatives, like *levitate*, *level* and *elevator*, to name a few. Syllabication does not allow the student to make those connections. In the word *circular* the syllable division divides the first syllable as cir, which then makes it difficult to make the connection to related words like *circle* and *circus*. You can watch a video of children describing the difference at: www.youtube.com/watch?v=Oc6O0lmQSFs.

Sidebar: Nonsense words during intervention
Are nonsense words nonsensical?

In the dyslexia community, it is common to use pseudowords and words with illegal letter strings (sequences of letters that will not occur in English) (e.g. shum) for two reasons. One is to assess how well a student can use their current reading skills to decode (or pronounce, since these assessments are done orally) words that are unfamiliar and use the score as one factor to determine if dyslexia is present (Gottardo *et al.*, 1999). The second reason is to require students to decode pseudowords during an intervention as a tool to teach reading (Dilberto *et al.*, 2009). The pseudowords in both circumstances range from monosyllabic to polysyllabic, and many of the words appear to be letter strings that would never occur in English. Additionally, in some cases, the graphemes are impossible to pronounce without knowing the etymology, and the meaning, of the word. For example, it is impossible to know how to pronounce any word with the digraph <ch> out of context. The Gottardo *et al.* study states that *have* is an irregular word, which is false—the word *have* has an <e> to prevent the word from ending in <v> as in words like *love, dove* and *shove*. Additionally, the polysyllabic words included on these assessments are especially misguided due to the effect stress has on the pronunciation and reading of words out of context, which makes reading words in isolation almost impossible.

Digraph: Two letters that are used together to create a grapheme that represents one phoneme.

If we look at the miscues that students make on nonsense word tasks, we can see that they might be attempting to find meaning in their language by misreading the nonsense words as real words. Reading is a meaning-making process; they are looking for the sense of the word, which is usually provided by either context or morphology, and nonsense words provide neither.

Nonword	Miscue	Orthographic similarity	Miscue as real word
weaf	wolf	Yes	Yes
mact	mark	Yes	Yes
teap	tape	Yes	Yes
prot	prote	Yes	No
peg	pug	Yes	Yes
ral	rail	Yes	Yes
pu	up	Yes	Yes
faw	fail	Partial	Yes
pu	pa	Yes	No
shum	shump	Yes	No
dat	bat	Yes	Yes
nup	dump	Partial	Yes
dess	dress	Yes	Yes
poth	pot	Yes	Yes
mo	om	Yes	No
nad	nade	Yes	No
dat	bat	Yes	Yes
mib	mid	Yes	Yes
skad	sad	Yes	Yes

Source: Adapted from TOWRE-2 (Torgesen, Wagner and Rashotte, 2012)

In teacher trainings, we often ask, "How do you pronounce the letter string *<chom>?" The answer we always get is /ʧɑm/. The problem with this is that the correct answer is, really, we can't know what the correct pronunciation is until we know what the word is. In the case of a digraph like <ch> the meaning and etymology of the word will drive the phonology. Etymology drives pronunciation, so how can a student know which is correct without context and meaning?

Here is an example of misguided nonsense word instruction in spelling. In this lesson the student was dictated a list of real words that then veered into the nonsense-word territory. What happened during this lesson is not inconsequential; it is confusing to students. Here is the list of words that were dictated with their IPA transcription. Take a look at the list and think about where it might be difficult and confusing to a group of struggling students.

Teacher pronunciation	Expected spelling
[ræt]	rat
[reɪt]	rate
[reɪtɪŋ]	rating
[rætɪŋ]	ratting
[bætɪŋ]	batting
[beɪtɪŋ]	*bating
[boʊtɪŋ]	*boting
[bɑpt]	bopped
[hɑpt]	hopped
[hɪpt]	hipped
[haɪpt]	*hiped

Do you see the conundrum with the starred words? The words were being dictated with no context. There was no conversation about what they meant. They were spelling based on phonology first. Yes, the lesson was focusing on how to spell words with a long and a short vowel. However, when the students spelled *<bating>, *<boting> and *<hiped> they were praised for being correct. What are they going to do when they spell *boating* as *<boting> and *baiting* as *<bating> and *hyped* as *<hiped>? Without meaning and context, we cannot spell.

How to use this book

This book is not intended to introduce you to a new approach or a new program for kids with dyslexia. The purpose of this book is to explain why spelling is so difficult for students with dyslexia and to dispel some common misunderstandings about the English writing system with examples from the language itself. The content of this book is intended to equip you with knowledge and activities that will help guide your instruction during teachable moments. The pictures and examples in this book are set in a handwriting font to demonstrate that you don't need anything but paper, pens/pencils, dictionaries and maybe the internet to teach your student how the English writing system works. Please use it as a resource that you can refer to time and again while teaching your students the sense and eloquence of the English writing system. I hope that as you make your way through this book the elegance and sense becomes more and more apparent and that you will fall in love with it the way I did or, better yet, that you help your students fall in love with it.

What to expect from this book

Chapter 1 will take a close look at the writing samples of students with dyslexia. The misspellings in those writing samples will be analyzed to help us understand what the student understands about English they need to learn. In other words, the writing sample is providing insight into the instructional needs of the students.

Chapter 2 will describe the steps a teacher and students can take to understand the spelling of a word and its word family. An explanation of the process will include identifying free and bound bases and how to identify those bases.

Chapter 3 includes several different instructional tips to help students study spellings that may be problematic for many different reasons. This chapter is set up so that you can go straight to the pattern that is being studied in the moment and find a useful instructional strategy.

Chapter 4 includes teaching tips that can used in the general education classroom.

CHAPTER 1

Show Me the Writing Sample

Words finally make sense to me.

Fourth grade (year 5) student

Early on in my career I used to say, "Just show me the writing sample." I was not as knowledgeable about dyslexia and language as I am now, but instinctively, it seemed like the most obvious place to go to find out what the student understands about how the English writing system works. To this day, I repeat the mantra, "You can find everything you need to know about the student's current understanding in their writing sample." While scores on standardized tests can provide information about general weaknesses and strengths and offer a way to monitor progress, they really are only a moment in time and the scores derived from them are subject to so many factors. When it comes to spelling, and reading, what the speller understands about how their own language really works will influence how they interact with it. Below are some writing samples and reading miscues from students with dyslexia ranging from second grade (year 3) to high school (years 10–13). While you read through the misspelling and miscues and what they tell us, remember that understanding them is not just a tool to help a student improve spelling, but it can also improve reading (Berninger *et al.*, 2010).

Braden, fourth grade (year 5)

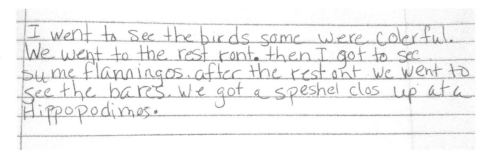

I went to see the birds some were colerful. We went to the rest ront. then I got to see sume flanningos. after the rest ont we went to see the bares. We got a speshel clos up at a Hippopodimes.

Braden has a lot to be proud of in this writing sample. He actually wrote quite a bit and his ideas are coherent and follow a logical order.

However, there are some observations about his spelling mistakes that can inform our instruction better than cold, hard test results.

- He is able to "sound out" words efficiently. This is evidence that he actually has strong phonemic understanding.

- The misspellings also provide evidence that the main strategy this student uses to spell is the "sound-it-out" strategy. As you learned in the opening sandwich-instruction activity, that strategy falls apart pretty quickly.

- The misspelling of *restaurant* as *<restront> is fascinating. When American English speakers pronounce the word *restaurant* it has two spoken syllables, so Braden is representing the two spoken syllables in his spelling.

- The misspelling of *some* as *<sume> is more evidence that Braden is spelling by sound, but the addition of the final *e* does not seem to have a purpose in his spelling. It is possible that he sounded out the first part of the word and then relied on visual memory, which led him to adding the silent *e*. In fact, it would be interesting to ask him why he added the *e*, which would lead us to the conversation about the several jobs of final *e*.

- The misspelling of *bears* as *<bares> provides an opportunity to talk about *homophones*.

- Braden's misspelling of *close* as *<clos> is another indication he needs to discover the several jobs of the single silent *e*.

> A homophone is a word that is pronounced
> in the same way as another word but has
> a different meaning (e.g. **see** and **sea**)
> and often a different spelling.

Brian, fifth grade (year 6)

brandish
hine teen
exspect - expect
shere - sure
enuf - enough

vnunifi - unify
electrishiti - electricity

The spelling mistakes this student makes inform us of the following.

- He is able to "sound out" words efficiently. He is using reasonable graphemes to represent the phonemes he is identifying in the words. This is evidence that he actually has strong phonemic understanding.

- Brian's misspellings also provide evidence that the only strategy he uses to spell is the "sound-it-out" strategy.

- This student needs to understand that final English suffixes do not end in <i>, which is illustrated by his spelling of the word *unify* as *< ununifi>.

- The misspelling of *electricity* is interesting. We could help the student understand the correct spelling simply by looking at related words like *electric*. Once he sees that he will understand why *electricity* is spelling with a <c> and not an <sh>. This could actually lead to a rich investigation when the word *electrician* is also included and the pronunciation shift of <c> from /c/ in electricity to /ʃ/ is noticed by the student.

Jason, eighth grade (year 9)

> to day we went over to freds.
> then I cout a crab.
> to day. I went skimbording and
> cot a fish.
> I had to meny cas to bay.
> I mad a sftboe blanck.
> thar was a big shorBrak
> ther was a masiv Sting ray.
> I Srft a smol wave
> we ate crab fo diner
> I grabd a Sting ray.

- Like Brian, Jason is able to "sound out" words efficiently as evidenced by the spelling of *many* as *<meny>, *boarding* as *<bording> and *massive* as *<masiv>. He has decent phonemic understanding.

- Jason needs to learn or be reminded that spoken syllables need to have a written vowel. In the word *surfed* which he spelled *<srft> he has the phonemes represented but failed to include at least one vowel. A conversation about which vowel should be used in the instance of the base in this word, which is *surf*, would be a conversation that included etymology and phonology. When Jason spelled <-ed> with a <t> he was representing what he heard, but he did not think about the meaning that <-ed> adds to the word *surfed* in the context he used it. We just have to switch the question we ask him from what does it sound like to what meaning are you trying to add to the word? There is much more about this type of question in the Chapter 3.

A sight word is a word that is usually taught as "irregular" and the student has to use memorization techniques to remember it (e.g. *sign, two*).

- The word *many* is often taught as a sight word that needs to be memorized. But it is clear that this technique has not worked for this student, so he needs to learn why *many* is spelled with an <a> and not an <e> to help him understand instead of memorize. In this case, the pronunciation of *many* was influenced by the word *any*.

- Jason spelled *too* as <to>, which could lead to a really informative discussion about homophones and why we spell *to, too* and *two* the way we do—the real orthographic reasons. You can find a lesson on this topic in a grade 1 (year 2) class and other videos of related instruction at: https://blogs.zis.ch/dallen/2014/09/24/thank-you-pete-bowers.

- The word *massive* is a great example of how we could teach Brian about the suffix of <-ive> and that a complete English word never ends in <v>, never. If you are thinking of the word *rev*, well *rev* is a clip, or a shortened form, of *revolution*. Once a student understands this it seems that it would easier for them to spell words in the future because they understand the spelling pattern and don't have to try to memorize every individual word.

What do reading miscues tell us?

Although this is a book about spelling, an understanding of spelling can also lead to better reading (Moats, 2005/6) because once a student understands how words are actually structured, they can look for those structures and then understand how to read/pronounce the words. There is more about how to help with this in Chapter 3.

Bianca, sixth grade (year 7)

Below is a list of reading miscues that Bianca made while reading. The first word listed is the word she pronounced and the second word is the target word she read.

party for pretty	got for get	from for of	indy for idea
how for now	ranging for rangers	invitated for invention	slipped for shipped
added for aided	rippened for ripened	farmer for family	previously for poverty
convicted for convinced	credentials for conditions	powerful for peaceful	lunged for lugged
sprinter for splintered	barrier for barren	shells for shoals	approximately for approaching
enter for invert	battle for battered		

Many of Bianca's mistakes reveal a tendency to guess at the words based on the shape of the word and its beginning letters. For the most part her guesses are not going to help her with comprehension, because the substituted words change the meaning of the sentence or clause being read. For example, substituting *party* for *pretty* is substituting a noun for an adjective. This is evidence that she is also not monitoring her comprehension.

Quantitative data is a simple and quick way to determine how a student is performing in comparison to their peers. And if we take a look at the word *quantitative* we can determine that the base is <quant> which means how much, how great and/or what amount (Harper, 2001–2019). However, if we look at the qualitative data, like spelling mistakes and reading miscues, we have a different lens into the student's current understanding and how it should inform our instruction. The spelling and reading miscues addressed in this chapter are indicators of what the students need to learn to use the words they have in their vocabulary now; they do not need to wait to fall within a predetermined scope and sequence or developmental stage. The evidence for this is that they use the words correctly. Spelling instruction should respond to the student's current needs.

CHAPTER 2

Word Investigations

One way to teach an accurate understanding of English spelling, in any teaching situation, is to study words using an approach that includes studying how morphology, etymology and phonology interact in English spellings (Bowers *et al.*, 2010) using word sums and lexical matrices. There are several steps in this process that can help students understand the spelling of the studied word and its relatives.

The words you and your student choose to study can be found everywhere, from conversations with the student/s to analyzing the students' misspellings and investigating those words. For example, the following chart is a list of spelling mistakes made by students with dyslexia.

Misspelled word	Phonemic transcription of attempted word	Attempted word
kisst	/kɪst/	kissed
lovd	/lʌvd/	loved
vacashun	/veɪkeɪʃən/	vacation
sine	/saɪn/	sign
tow	/tu/	two
ben	/bɪn/	been

An initial step to the word investigation might be to go through a list of misspelled words, like the one above, and allow the student to notice how similar their spelling is to the pronunciation of the word (remember the IPA symbols are symbols, not letters) and how that differs from the spelling of the word. This can lead into a conversation about the importance of understanding what the word means, and how it is built, before thinking about how it is pronounced. Below the process of how to uncover the meaning, structure and pronunciation of words is described.

Revealing underlying word structure

To begin, let's study the word *vacation*. The student's misspelling of *vacation* is *<vacashun>, which presents some evidence that the student is spelling by sound first and is not thinking about how morphology, semantics or syntax affect a spelling. The misspelling also reveals a misunderstanding of the affixes that are added to a bound base. What follows is an example of an investigation of *vacation*, which will use the inquiry process to help a student discover the structure of a word and thereby understand the spelling.

1. What does the word mean?

At this step, ask the student to think about what the word *vacation* means. If the student does not know the meaning of the word, look it up in a dictionary or have them use it in a sentence. It might be that they know what it means, or how to use it, but they cannot articulate the definition. If you look at the dictionary on an Apple computer, *vacation* is defined as an extended period of recreation, especially one spent away from home or in traveling. It is important that the word that is under investigation is a known word because it isn't really prudent to have students spell words they don't know.

Most people do not write words they do not know, in fact, there is not one word in this book of which I do not know the meaning. Before you get started the graphic below from www.wordworkskingston.com is a helpful tool to have handy during this inquiry process.

Found an interesting word?

1. **What is the sense and meaning of your word?**

2. **How is it built?**

   ↕ Can you identify any bases or affixes with a word sum?

3. **What related words can you find?**

   • **Morphological relatives:** Look for words that share a base.

   • **Etymological relatives:** Look for words that share a history.

4. **What graphemes function coherently here?**

   • Check that they represent the phonemes across the morphological family.

   • Check the influence of word origin on grapheme choice.

   • Is what you thought was a grapheme actually an orthographic marker?

---

2. How is it built?

Once the student has demonstrated that they have at least a basic understanding of the meaning of the word, they are now ready to make a hypothesis about the structure of the word. This is when a word sum will be very helpful. The student suggests a word sum for *vacation* using the morphemic boundary notation (+) and the process arrow (which can be announced as *becomes*) (→) to reveal their hypothesis of the underlying structure. The morphemes in the word *vacation* are:

vace + ate + ion → vacation

which reveals that <vace> is a bound base, which means it cannot be a word on its own until it is fixed to another base or an affix. The final non-syllabic *e* is proposed to be on the end of the bound base because if it was not present the <c> would double in the final iteration of the word and become *<vaccation> (see the "When to double a consonant" section in Chapter 3). Once the word sum is hypothesized, the student reads it out loud, morpheme by morpheme while including a slight pause where the morpheme boundary notation (+) is to signal that they understand there is a boundary there. To add a multisensory component to the word sum the student can trace the morphemes with their finger and announce the morphemes at the same time. Another way to accomplish this is to write the morphemes on separate cards so the student is manipulating the cards as they read the morphemes. The base and affixes can be on separate color cards to further signal the different functions of each morpheme. There is more on how this can be done in Chapter 3.

Now the student has to prove that their word sum is correct and, in order for them to do that, they have to identify at least one other English word with the affixes of <-ate> and <-ion>, the affixes identified in the word sum (the word *activate* has an <-ate> and the <-ion> in *action* would satisfy this requirement). Remember, at this step in the process the student is not yet focused on the phonology of the word; they are still investigating its morphological structure (how the word is built).

3. What are its relatives?

Now that the student has an understanding of the morphological structure of the word, they are ready to begin investigating words related to *vacation* in both spelling and meaning to help further their understanding. With some guidance from you, if needed, students at this step can either generate a list of words that are related in spelling and meaning or they can search for related words at www.neilramsden. co.uk/spelling/searcher. If they enter the bound base <vace> (without the proposed e) the following partial list of words is generated: *vacant, vacate, evacuee, vacuous, vacantly, vacating, vacantly, vacation, evacuation*, etc. Students can then use an etymology resource, like the one at www.etymonline.com, to determine if the <vace> base is related to each of the words listed. In the case of the base <vace> we can check the words *vacant* and *vacation* to see if they share the same history and meaning. To do this we have to confirm that they share a meaning, a spelling and an etymology.

You can see from the entries below from www.etymonline.com that both *vacation* and *vacant* share a meaning and a history. However, be careful, when looking for words with the same base: the word *vaccination* could be suggested by a student, because on the surface it looks like it has the same base. We can pretty easily determine that the meaning is not the same, but it wouldn't be unreasonable for a student to make the hypothesis that to vaccinate someone is to remove or empty the disease. When we look at the etymological entry for *vaccination* below, we see that there is not a connection between *vacation* and *vaccinate* so they do not belong in the same lexical matrix.

vacation (n.)

late 14c., "freedom from obligations, leisure, release" (from some activity or occupation), from Old French *vacacion* "vacancy, vacant position" (14c.) and directly from Latin *vacationem* (nominative *vacatio*) "leisure, freedom, exemption, a being free from duty, immunity earned by service," noun of state from past participle stem of *vacare* "be empty, free, or at leisure," from PIE *wak-*, extended form of root *eue-* "to leave, abandon, give out."

vacant (adj.)

c. 1300, "not filled, held, or occupied," from Old French *vacant* "idle, unoccupied" (of an office, etc.), from Latin *vacantem* (nominative *vacans*), "empty, unoccupied," present participle of *vacare* "be empty," from PIE *wak-*, extended form of root *eue-* "to leave, abandon, give out." Meaning "characterized by absence of mental occupation" is from 1570s. Related: *Vacantly*.

vaccination (n.)

1800, used by British physician Edward Jenner (1749–1823) for the technique he devised of preventing smallpox by injecting people with the cowpox virus (*variolae vaccinae*), from *vaccine* adj.) "pertaining to cows, from cows" (1798), from Latin *vaccinus* "from cows," from *vacca* "cow," a word of uncertain origin. "The use of the term for diseases other than smallpox is due to Pasteur" [OED].

Source: Harper, 2001–2019

(Note: It is important to remember that this resource is about etymology only; it does not reveal morphology.)

Once it has been determined that the words are all related in meaning, spelling and etymology, the words can be added to the lexical matrix. Now, the student can also write the word sums using morphological boundary markers and a process arrow. The matrix and the word sums allow the students to separate the morphemes, identify grammatical functions of suffixes and understand meaning shifts based on morphemes. The word sums can be done before or after a matrix. The matrix can be created at the mini-matrix maker: www.neilramsden.co.uk/spelling/matrix/temp/index.html or you can create a matrix with a pen and paper.

		ant	ly		
		ate	ing		
e	\<vace\>		ion		
		u	ate		ion
				ee	

Word sums:

vace + ate + ion → vacation

vace + ate + ion + s → vacations

e + vace + u + ate → evacuate

e + vace + u + ate + ion → evacuation

vace + ant + ly → vacantly

vace + ant → vacant

e + vace + u + ee → evacuee

vace + ate + ing → vacating

4. How is the word pronounced?

Now we have enough information about the structure of the word and its relatives to start the conversation about phonology. In this step the student should study the matrix while pronouncing the words. During this process ask the student to verbalize any phonological shifts they notice within the word family. For example, in the word *vacate* the <t> is generally pronounced as /t/ but when the suffix <-ion> is added the <t> shifts its pronunciation to /ʃ/. The student might notice that in the word *evacuee* the vowel <a> is pronounced /æ/ and in *vacation* the vowel <a> is pronounced /eɪ/. This observation is important for the student to notice and verbalize so they can begin to understand that we can change the way we pronounce a word but not the way we spell it.

Let's try that inquiry process with a free base

Many students who struggle with spelling will spell the word *does* as *<dose>. But when they learn the structure of the word and why it cannot be spelled that way, they understand it. The word *does* ends up on sight-word lists pretty frequently and it might be surprising to learn that there is a suffix on this word. Let's see if we can figure out the sense of *does* so the student develops an understanding.

1. What does the word mean?

I think we can agree that most students will understand what *does* means, but they might have a hard time defining it. So, in this case having the student use the word in a sentence might be the best way to confirm they understand the word.

2. How is it built?

does (v.)

third-person singular present indicative of do (v.), originally a Northumbrian variant in Old English that displaced doth, doeth in literary English 16c.–17c.

Source: Harper, 2001–2019

Remember, this is when the student makes a hypothesis about the structure of the word using a word sum. The student suggests a word sum using the morphemic boundary notation (+) and the process arrow (which can be announced as becomes) (→) to reveal the underlying structure of the word. In the case of *does* you and your student might be stumped, so take a moment to study the structure of the word and see if you notice any common suffixes. If that doesn't help, try to think of other words with a similar structure (e.g. *goes*). Once you have done that, your student will probably be ready with a hypothesis that looks like this:

do + es → does

3. What are its relatives?

Now is the time to start brainstorming. What other words have the same base and the same meaning and/or function? There are not many in this case, but they are: *doing* and *done*. You might be questioning the <-ne> in *done* as a suffix that can be removed to reveal the <do> base, but there is an explanation. The <-ne> suffix is called a non-productive suffix. This means that historically it was affixed to words, but it is no longer used to build present-day English. In order to provide evidence to support that <-ne> is a suffix, we have to find at least one other word with the same suffix. How about *gone*, which has the base <go> and the suffix <-ne>? That is the proof we need that our hypothesis is probably correct. Now we are ready to put *does* into a matrix.

<do>	es
make, act, perform, cause	ing
	ne

4. How is the word pronounced?

The phonology shifts in this matrix are interesting. The student will notice that the pronunciation of the base word vowel shifts but the spelling does not, just like in *vacation*; this is a key concept in understanding spelling. We can see the shift with the phonemic transcriptions:

does

dʌz

doing

duɪŋ

done

dʌn

The <do> base changes its phonology when the affix <-ing> is added. The affixes on *vacation* changed the phonology of the word when they were fixed on to each other. The phonology of words and reading is an interesting, and important, piece of the puzzle for spelling and students will notice if guided by this inquiry process.

Is this appropriate for young students?

Yes, and to illustrate that point, the videos listed below include young children learning the structure of English.

- The teacher in this video takes a young kindergarten (year 1) class through the word family *rain*: https://vimeo.com/189070725.

- This video shows students in first grade (year 2) investigating graphemes of words in the context of word sums. The importance of spelling out the words in digraphs and trigraphs is illustrated by Dr. Peter Bowers: www.youtube.com/watch?v=UeNnLwNzlkU.

- In this video kindergarten (year 1) students learn about word sums and the lexical matrix: www.youtube.com/watch?v=VW8in2AlPy8&t=5s.

Is this inquiry process "Structured Literacy"?

You bet it is. It is multisensory, it is structured and it is very explicit. The student participates as a word investigator through a scientific inquiry process. The student announces the word sums while tracing the letters and then explains why and how they suggested their hypothesis for the spelling of the word. They study morphology, etymology and phonology. The student has to notice grammatical shifts which affect syntax and semantics. What's even better is this type of instruction can be used in any situation, not just an intervention situation. It might be worthwhile to study the structure of mathematical, scientific and grammar words. What would happen to a student's understanding of math if they studied how *denominator* is built or how *biology* is built? You can find activities for content area lessons in Chapter 4.

CHAPTER 3

Teachable Moments

Oh, so the longer the word is, the more meaning it has?!

Sixth grade (year 7) student

A rhyming family is a list of words that rhyme, like **rat, bat, cat,** etc. A word family is a collection of words that are related in meaning and spelling, like **act, acts, react, action,** etc.

Teachable moments are the best time and place to study spelling. These moments can come up at any time while studying any topic. Words like *denominator, addition* and *sum,* can come up during math instruction and then next session the words *plot, action* and *writing* can come during a conversation about literature at any age. The rest of this book is designed to allow you to search for a specific spelling topic that will include an example of how to help students discover the answers to the questions about words that they are studying. Studying words is most effective when done in the context of a *word family* (not a *rhyming family*). A rhyming family can go quickly awry. For example, the following words rhyme: *ate, bait, weight, state*, but a child with dyslexia would have to memorize each word, even though they rhyme, because rhyming does not guarantee that they will be spelled alike. But if we study word families (e.g. *act, acts, action*) the student can be sure that the base will be spelled the same. There are some patterns that can be investigated by searching for spelling similarities in unrelated words, instead of memorizing rules. Some examples are f, l, s and z (stuff, fell, dress and buzz) spellings at the end of base words, the ck/k (trick and silk) spelling, the tch/ch (match and bunch) spelling and so on. So, the activities listed below are designed to help the student study the patterns and make the discoveries and connections on their own, with your guidance. Make sure to give the students the time they need to process the information and allow them to be wrong. This type of instruction can be powerful when wrong answers are investigated as much as when right answers are applauded.

Paths to discovery
Understanding "silent letters" or orthographic markers

Orthographic markers are letters or letter combinations that, may or may not, represent phonology, in other words, they seem to be "silent" letters. English words that don't appear to follow any phonics rules, or can't be sounded out, are often labeled as irregular or sight words, and students are told that the words are crazy and the only way to study them is to memorize them. However, there is evidence that it might be more effective to teach students early on that there is a reason for the spelling of words like *two* (Devonshire, Morris and Fluck, 2013; Bowers and Bowers, 2017).

■ DISCOVERY ACTIVITY

Two

The word *two* can be explicitly taught and understood by students. Often students will spell this word *<tow>. Begin by asking the student what the word means. If needed, have them use the word in a sentence. Then ask them if they can think of other words that are related in meaning and spelling. The key is looking for related words to discover the patterns.

Discovery questions

- Why is the spelling of this word difficult for you to understand?

- What do you notice about all of these words in the list we generated?

- How are these words related in meaning?

- Can you now describe why there is a <w> in <two>?

Below is a chart of the investigative process (this is not an exhaustive list of the words that can be included in this chart).

	Related words	Are the words related in meaning?
two	twice	Yes
	twin	Yes
	between	Yes
	twilight	Yes
	twenty	Yes

People

Another example of a so-called sight word is the word *people,* which can also be understood through a discovery process. Often students with dyslexia will spell this word *<peple> or *<pepol> or another variation, because they are trying to represent all the phonemes they hear and feel, and they might add an <o> because they know they've seen an <o> in that word but they don't have an understanding of the entire spelling.

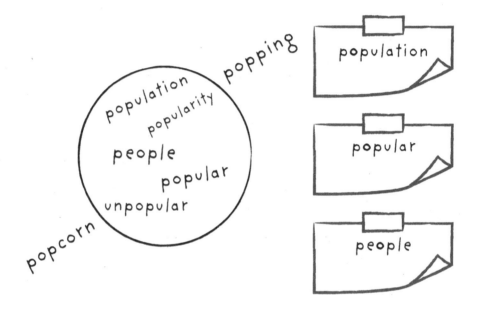

■ DISCOVERY ACTIVITY

As always, we start with making sure the student understands the meaning of *people.* For this word we can then check the etymology (e.g. at www.etymonline.com) of *people,* which will reveal that it is derived from the Latin *populous.* During the conversation you, or your student/s, can compile the list of words the student suggests might be related to *people.* Some words that the student might suggest are: *popular* and *population*. It is also possible, even probable, that the student will suggest a word that doesn't fit, like the word *popped*. This is a very good mistake that leads to a discussion about why it does not fit. For example, the word *popped* does not fit because, even though it sounds like *popular*, we have to remember that the words also have to share a meaning.

Discovery questions

- Why is the spelling of this word difficult for you to understand?

- What is unexpected about the spelling?

- What do you notice about all of these words in the list we generated?

- How are these words related in meaning?

- Can you explain why there is an <o> in people?

Examples of other sight words that can be investigated: sign, does, goes, etc.

Make it multisensory

Some students need more hands-on activities to help them understand a new concept and commit it to memory. We can make a lesson multisensory by providing more ways for the student to either manipulate cards, write different concepts in different colors, spell words out loud or tap morphemes with their fingers or down their arm. These are just a few ways to incorporate multisensory strategies into a lesson.

Discovering the form and function of affixes
Inflectional suffixes

Young children understand inflectional suffixes pretty early—just think about their ability to differentiate between *cat* and *cats* and *walk* and *walked* when they are learning to talk. They understand that by adding /s/ to /cæt/ they are creating a plural. They also understand that when they add /t/ to <wɔk> they are creating a past tense. Additionally, they understand that adding /s/ to a verb like /wɔk/ creates a third person singular. They know this because they understand their own language. What they might not have been explicitly taught is that, in spelling, we represent the past tense of the word *walk* with an <-ed> and not a <t>, but they may spell the word as *<walkt> because they are sounding it out instead of thinking about meaning first. Discovering the affixes and their functions can be helpful.

■ DISCOVERY ACTIVITY

Generating lists of words with similar spellings, like the examples of inflectional suffixes below, can help students discover the function of those suffixes. Let's take a look at the following words:

play, plays, playing, played

To start this activity, have the student identify the base word and the suffix. Then have the student use each word in a sentence. After each sentence, have the student identify the function of each inflectional suffix. For example, the suffix <-s> either creates a verb ("She plays in the water") or it creates a noun ("She was in several Broadway plays last year"). The suffix <-ed>, in this example, creates a past tense ("She played with her friend yesterday"). The suffix <-ing> can create a present participle ("She is playing with her friend"). The function will depend on the sentences your student generates, so be careful to consider carefully how the word is being used—the <-ed> is not always a past tense and the <-ing> is not always a present participle. Context is everything.

Make it multisensory

Write the base on a card and write the inflectional suffixes on different colored cards. Then have the student use additional cards to label the morphemes.

Derivational suffixes

Derivational suffixes create new words. To help students discover the form and function of these suffixes, choose a word that you and your student/s are studying or a word (or spelling pattern) that you know your student is struggling with. For this example, let's revisit the word investigation into *act* that was presented earlier.

■ DISCOVERY ACTIVITY

Begin by listing words built on the base chosen for study; in this case the base is <act>.

act, action, reactive, active, activate

Create word sums for each word and then label each morpheme to indicate its form and its function. Make sure the word is not studied out of context. For example, the word *action* could be a noun ("His actions were pure") or an adjective ("We went to an action movie").

Discovery questions

- What does *act* mean?

- Can you think of other words that are related in meaning and spelling?

- Can you use each word in a sentence?

- Can you identify each suffix?

- Can you identify the function of each suffix using the sentence you created using that word? Did the suffix change the function of the base?

Let's investigate some of the derivational suffixes and see what we discover. An <-ion> suffix can create a noun as illustrated with the word *action* ("There was a lot of action in that game"). In other words the <-ion> can also create a verb ("We have to ration the food"). We can also add an <-ive> suffix and build the word *active*, which can function as an adjective and then add an <-ly> to get *actively*, which is an adverb. Derivational suffixes add meaning and often change grammatical function of words and bases. When we ask the student what the word means and guide them to hypothesize how the suffix can change the meaning, we help the student learn to analyze words and morphemes to help them understand the structure. Studying words, especially to understand spelling, out of context is problematic.

Make it multisensory

Write the base on a card. Use a different colored card to write the suffix. Then use cards to label the base and the function of the suffix.

Sentence the student used: *He is an active child.*

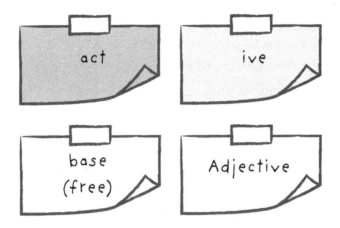

Prefixes

Many words with suffixes also have prefixes and some words only have prefixes. For the base <act> we can add the prefix <re> to build the word *react*. This word sets up for an interesting conversation about the meaning of the prefix <re> added to the base, which is *back to the original place* (Harper, 2001–2019). But it also leads to an important conversation about morpheme boundaries. When we do a word sum for *react* we get the structure of re + act → react, which reveals that the <e> and the <a> are part of different morphemes. In terms of reading, this is a significant discovery, because struggling readers will often read the word as if the grapheme <ea>, like in *lead*, is present in *react*. The addition of <re> to the base <act> creates a verb, but if we make the word more complex and add the <-ion> suffix, we have created a noun with:

$$re + act + ion → reaction$$

▪ DISCOVERY ACTIVITY

To help a student discover prefixes you can work through this discovery activity. The goal of the activity is for you to guide the student to the discovery by using the questions that are listed. Resist the urge to provide the answer and allow the student to make mistakes. Be sure to choose words to study that the student uses in their spoken vocabulary.

Discovery questions

- Where do you add a prefix—at the beginning or end of the word? If they do not know, investigating the word prefix (pre + fix → prefix) could be helpful.

- Can you think of other prefixes that you can add to this base?

- How do those other prefixes change the meaning of the word?

Make it multisensory

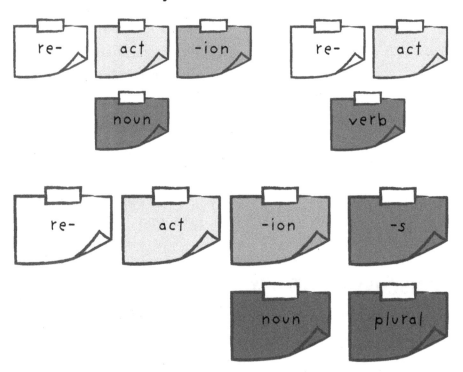

Connecting vowels

We can't talk about discovering affixes without also discovering connecting vowels and their role in spelling. The base <act> is a good place to find a connecting vowel. When we build the word *actually* we reveal this structure:

$$act + u + al + ly \rightarrow actually$$

The student can discover that the <u> is there to connect morphemes within a word. See the glossary for more about connecting vowels.

Spellings revealed by word sums

When to double a consonant

In many word sums affixes end with <e> on the left side of the word sum but the <e> is not present on the right side of the word sum.

$$take + ing \rightarrow taking$$

This word sum can be announced the following way:

t-a-k-e plus *ing* becomes ($\rightarrow$) t-a-k replace the *e, ing*

The graphemes and marker letters are announced in the base, and affixes are announced as a unit and not individual graphemes. To see this spelling out or writing out loud in action watch this link: www.wordworkskingston.com/WordWorks/Spelling-Out_Word_Sums.html.

This is one reason why it is imperative that word sums use a process arrow and not an equal sign; the underlying structure of the word on the left-hand side of the word sum is often not the same as the right-hand side of the word sum.

This is the suffixing process to check for spelling changes to the base and the suffixes.

1. The student will check the morpheme boundaries for a single, non-syllabic, silent *e* at the end of the previous morpheme.

2. If there is one, they check the following morpheme to see if it begins with a vowel. If so, the previous *e* is replaced by the following morpheme, usually an affix. Let's use *taking* as the example:

$$take + ing \rightarrow taking$$

3. Let's take a look at what happens when there is not a single, silent, non-syllabic *e*:

$$bat + ing \rightarrow batting$$

$$chip + ed \rightarrow chipped$$

▧ DISCOVERY

When a base ends with a vowel and a consonant following that vowel and the suffix begins with a vowel, the final consonant doubles.

Changing y to i suffixing convention

Have you ever seen a list of words like this?

cried, tried, fried, dried

Instead of teaching these words as bases with an <-ed> suffix, they are taught as complete words, which is a huge missed opportunity to show students that the <ie> in these words are not actually diagraphs or vowel teams. Instead, they are the result of a suffixing convention. Let's look at some word sums to reveal the true underlying structure of these words:

$$cry + ed \rightarrow cried$$

$$try + ed \rightarrow tried$$

$$fry + ed \rightarrow fried$$

$$dry + ed \rightarrow dried$$

Discovery questions

- What do you notice?

- Do you see a pattern emerging?

- Can you describe the pattern you notice?

▓ DISCOVERY

If the base ends with a <y> and the suffix begins with a vowel, the <y> changes to an <i>. So the <i> is really part of the base and the <-ed> is the suffix. These are actually words with two morphemes. Hmm, so maybe now *cries* and *tries* are coming to mind. If we use the same description we used for the previous words for these new words, then we must end up with the following word sums.

$$cry/i + es \rightarrow cries$$

$$try/i + es \rightarrow tries$$

$$fry/i + es \rightarrow fries$$

$$dry/i + es \rightarrow dries$$

Discovering grapheme/phoneme options

Helping students understand phoneme/grapheme options can help them understand spelling. Most kids learn that <a> represents /æ/ without any consideration of the environment of that <a> and the reality that this is just one possible articulation of <a>. The environment of the grapheme <a> determines what phoneme it represents. For example, in the word *about* the first syllable is unstressed, which is articulated as a schwa. Below is a graphic of one way to represent the grapheme options of <a> that can only be discovered while studying the word. A graphic of <ch> is also included to illustrate that this can be done for all graphemes.

	/æ/ fat		/ʧ/ chip, child, much
<a>	/eɪ/ make	<ch>	/ʃ/ machine, chef
	/ə/ about		/k/ chord, choral, chemical
	/ɔ/ fall		

Trade in the letter wall for a phoneme wall

Almost every elementary school (years 2–6) classroom has an alphabet on the wall. On each letter card there is usually a picture of something that begins with the letter on the card. For example, the <a> is almost always accompanied by a picture of an apple, which is trying to convey that <a> represents /æ/, like in apple. The problem is that /æ/ is just one of many sounds that the grapheme <a> represents, so we are setting up the kids for confusion when they come to a word like *awake*.

Why not put phonemes on the wall and include the graphemes that students discover that represent those phonemes. They will notice these in their reading and just by observing words. It isn't uncommon to find the words on the lists below in kindergarten (year 1) reading and their oral vocabulary.

/e/ – ate		
<a_e>	<ai>	<ay>
take	tail	stay
lake	chain	pays
made	paid	today
evacuate		tray

The beauty of this is that students can add words as they come up over the entire course of the year and they start to look for and notice sound options for graphemes.

Use the other wall for graphemes

It might also be useful to put up a grapheme wall, like the following.

<y>			
/aɪ/	/i/	/j/	/ɪ/
my	baby	yes	hymn
type	busy	yummy	crystal
hydrant	lady	beyond	
	yummy		

The wall charts above can also be charts in students' notebooks, and they can add sheets for each new grapheme and phoneme they discover.

Double f, l, s and z

Remember the misspelled word *<speld>? This one can be easily explained. First, the student needs to identify the meaning of the word. So, let's say they use it in a sentence like, "I spelled the word wrong." Then they need to identify the morphemes and one way to do that is have them use the base in a sentence like "I don't want to spell it wrong," which in this case is <spell>. Now that they have discovered the base of the word we can talk about the spelling pattern of when to double an f, l, s or z. To do this, let's look at a few more words:

spell, tell, small, tall, mull, poll, still, quill

staff, bluff, stiff

pass, mess, kiss, cross, puss

buzz

Discovery questions

- Do you notice a pattern?

- Are there any other words you could include in this list?

- What is the pattern?

The objective here is to help the student notice the pattern on their own instead of providing the rule and then simply practicing it. I will give you the pattern below, and in the practical activities section later in the chapter I will describe one way to help students notice the pattern and then describe it.

Background information

When a base word ends in f, l, s or z and those graphemes are preceded by a single vowel, the grapheme doubles. What was tricky in the word spelled for this student was that they were not thinking about the word as two morphemes, so the pattern was missed because they were only listening for the final sound /d/ instead of thinking about the meaning of the word. You might have also noticed that I slipped in a <qu> with the word quill. It is important that students know this word follows the pattern because at first glance it looks like the <ui> could be the diagraph <ui>, like in the word build, but the <u> in quill is part of the grapheme <qu> and it is not functioning as a vowel in that word. It is also important to help students notice that this rule does not apply to suffixes, which is why words like wonderful and beautiful do not end in a double <l>, because the <l> is part of the suffix <-ful>, not the base.

Is it k or ck?

Spelling words that end in with the pronunciation of /k/ can be tricky until the student understands the pattern. See if you can spot the pattern after studying these words:

truck, silk, stick, drink, luck, quick

Background information

When a base word ends in /k/ and is preceded by one vowel, the spelling of /k/ will be <ck>. If the base words ends in /k/ and is directly preceded by a consonant the spelling of /k/ will be spelled with the grapheme <k>. Again, the difficult thing for spellers is that they have to remember to consider the base and not the affixes. In a word like *atomic*, the rule does not apply because the final /k/ is part of a suffix <-ic> not the base.

When to use <ch> and <tch>

You should be getting the hang of this by now, so try to find the pattern in these spellings:

catch, fetch, pinch, ditches, mulch, britches

You may have noticed that I threw in a few suffixes, but hopefully they did not throw you off too much. Here is the pattern: when the base of a content word ends in /tʃ/ and is preceded by one vowel, the spelling of /tʃ/ will be <tch>. If the base words ends in /tʃ/ and is directly preceded by a consonant the spelling of /tʃ/ will be <ch>. Again, the difficult thing for spellers is that they have to remember to consider the base and the not affixes when trying to determine the spelling. For example, in a word like *ditches* the student has to get to the base <ditch> to prevent spelling *ditches* as *<diches>.

■ PRACTICAL ACTIVITY

Descriptive generalizations

Students with dyslexia are often described as great problem solvers and pattern seekers, and I have also seen those strengths with my students. The English writing system is loaded with patterns just waiting to be discovered. One way to empower students to notice and understand those patterns is to teach students to describe the patterns they notice. A descriptive generalization is a characterization (description) of spelling patterns that can be observed in the data; the data is the English language itself. The generalization should be written in a way that means anyone who reads it, who has never seen the data (English), will to be able to locate words that are completely consistent with the generalization. One way to accomplish this is to have the student play "Discover the spelling pattern."

Discover the spelling pattern

During this activity the student is presented with a list of words with a common spelling pattern of changing the <y> to an <i> when an affix is added. The student is tasked with discovering the spelling pattern on their own. The teacher does not teach the rule first because the purpose is for the student to discover the pattern through an investigation. The student then comes up with a descriptive generalization, in other words, they describe the pattern in their own words. The student can either verbalize the generalization or they can write it out on their own. The pictures below illustrate this activity with the <y> to <i> pattern and the f, l, s and z spelling pattern. Obviously, the student still has not fully completed the generalization and it needs revision, but that is part of the process. The student then spells words with that pattern and uses the description they created to see if it applies to the words spelled.

In the first description, the student attempted to spell the word *tried*, which she spelled as *<tryyed>. After she spelled it she was able to consult the generalization she created and noticed her mistake, which led to her being able to correct it independently.

To provide some support the student was given the sentence starter, "When a base words ends with..."; that is all the support this student received, and it was enough to allow her to write what she noticed.

If a word does not fit the generalization, the student is encouraged to look for other words that do not fit and come up with a new generalization for those words. For example, the words *played* and *strayed* do not fit in the first generalization but the student is encouraged to find another pattern that explains the spelling.

cry → cried   pattern

try → tried   starter

fry → fried   description:
                When a base word

tryted →   ends in a y
                when the suffix is
tryyed   a vowel you
                change it to a y.

Incorrect generalization

cry → cried   pattern

try → tried   starter

fry → fried   description:
                When a base word

tryted → ↑   ends in a y
                when the suffix is
tryyed   a vowel you
                change it to an i.

Corrected generalization

Discover the Pattern

bell

less

mass

stiff

spell

When the base word ends in l, s, f you double it and it has a short vowel.

---

f, l, s, and z

Discovering the function of the single, silent *e*

The single, silent *e* is almost always taught as having one role in English spelling: to make the previous vowel long. Yes, it does sometimes signal a previous long vowel (*make, joke, prone*), but that is just one function. Students who don't understand all the functions of the single, silent *e* will often add an *e* to the end of any word they think they misspelled. And if they perceive a long vowel sound in any word, they will add an *e*, and that falls apart almost immediately with words like *boat, team* and *raid*. So, let's dig in to this marker letter to see what else it does.

Marks a previous vowel as long:

strike, broke, cute

Marks a <c> as soft:

mice, chance, place

Marks a preceding vowel as stressed:

rationale, morale

Marks a <g> as soft:

judge, strange, huge

Cancels a plural:

please, dense, tense, lapse (without the final e, these words would be: pleas, dens, tens and laps; each are plural forms of other words)

Differentiates homophones:

bye, toe, awe

Prevents a word from ending in <v>:

love, dove, shove, glove

Prevents a word from ending in <u>:

plague, vague, continue

Marks a shift in phonology for <th> and also changes grammatical function:

teeth, teethe

bath, bathe

■ ACTIVITY

What is the reason?

To help students understand and verbalize the reasons for spellings, like the orthographic marker of the single silent *e*, you can write words on cards and have the student tell you the reason for the marker letter. As a variation, ask them to explain to you what the word would be, or how it would be pronounced, if the single silent *e* was not there.

tease

rice

fudge

love

bathe

There really is no such thing as a sight word

Words that don't appear to make sense on the surface usually end up on sight-word lists, no-excuse word lists and red-word lists, which all send the signal to the student that there is no sense to these words and they have to just memorize them. If we take a moment to take a deeper and more critical look at the words we deem as crazy, we might be able to notice the sense in the spellings. English isn't meant to be memorized, it's meant to be noticed and investigated. As practitioners, we've tried teaching students to memorize words, but even with the best techniques, they are not able to or it is extremely difficult. Most students with dyslexia will cram for a weekly spelling test, only to forget those words the next time they have to use them in context, or at all. But every word can be investigated and understood and that has to be more effective. There are so many spelling puzzles to solve with some guidance from you.

Here are steps to teach words that don't appear to make sense

Let's investigate the word *sign* and take a look at a visual representation, using a lexical matrix, to illustrate how to teach a student about real word families and how the pronunciation of a word can shift based on the morphemes that build the word. It is important to allow the students to notice the phonological shifts on their own and announce them to you.

		al	ling
de re	**\<sign\>**	ate	ion ure
		i	fy
		ing	

The students can also build word sums with the base \<sign\>. While they create these word sums, they announce each letter (not pronouncing the word yet) and when they get to the becomes arrow, they announce that the word *becomes* and they write the word as a whole. Below are three word sums of many that can be made from the matrix above.

sign + al → signal

sign + ate + ure → signature

de + sign + ate → designate

The function of the \<g\> in \<sign\> is revealed by studying related words.

Now that we have looked at how word investigations can reveal the structure of words, let's look at everything a student can learn from a word list built on just the one base that I have used throughout this book. The list of concepts discovered is after the list, and as you read through them remember that this could be what spelling lists in schools look like and accomplish. Instead of a memorization task, we have a meaning-making task that builds understanding and bypasses the cognitive load on working memory.

\<act\>

Spelling word	Word sum
acts	act + s → acts
active	act + ive → active
react	re + act → react
reactivate	re + act + ive + ate → reactivate
reaction	re + act + ion → reaction
actually	act + u + al + ly → actually
activate	act + ive + ate → activate
activated	act + ive + ate + ed → activated
activates	act + ive + ate + s → activates
inactive	in + act + ive → inactive
inactivate	in + act + ive + ate → inactivate
activating	act + ive + ate + ing → activating
enact	en + act → enact
enacts	en + act + s → enacts
deactivation	de + act + ive + ate + ion → deactivation
action	act + ion → action

A matrix is an invaluable tool to use with students when studying orthography. It organizes a family of words, built from a base, which are related in meaning, spelling and etymology. They include the base, prefixes, suffixes and connecting vowels but do not have to be comprehensive. They are meant to be fluid and added to as students discover new words that belong in the matrix. A matrix has to be read from left to right and columns cannot be skipped.

en in re	act	ion s		
		ive	ate	ed ing s
		u	al	ly

What did the students discover by not only spelling these words but also creating a word sum?

- That the final e of a base or suffix will drop when the following suffix begins with a vowel.

- A silent e at the end of a base or suffix, like in active, does not always signal a long vowel.

- The word actually reveals the presence of a connecting vowel.

- The <e> and the <a> in reactive do not create a digraph. Even more important is the understanding that the word react cannot have an <ea> digraph because graphemes never cross morphemic boundaries: re + act → react. The <e> grapheme is part of the prefix <re>, and the <a> grapheme is part of the base. They are two separate morphemes. This can be further illustrated with the word *hothouse*; we do not read that word with a <th> grapheme, because the two morphemes of <hot> and *house* are understood. The <t> and the <h> are separate graphemes in separate morphemes.

- The word sum for <actually> reveals why there are two <l>s: each <l> belongs to a different morpheme: <act> + <u> + <al> + <ly> → actually.

- The suffix is <-ion> not <-tion>. The evidence is in the word family:

  - action – act + ion

  - adoption – adopt + ion

  - eruption – e + rupt + ion.

With a logical spelling list like this, the student is not just learning how to spell the base <act>, but they are also becoming more familiar with common prefixes and affixes that they will find in thousands of other words. With a list like this, we can replace the practice of memorizing lists of unrelated words, which the struggling student is likely to forget two weeks later, with a list of related words with common affixes.

Now compare the <act> matrix on the previous page to this one from a third-grade (year-4) class:

1. petrified
2. disaster
3. psychiatrist
4. exemplary
5. overwrought
6. listless
7. nourishment
8. reluctance
9. distress
10. narrative

Bonus. Namatisit

On this list, there are no meaning connections made. No grammatical connections. No spelling patterns. It is a lesson in remote memorization that is likely to be forgotten by the student with dyslexia within a week.

CHAPTER 4

Teaching Tips

When in doubt, spell it out

When students with dyslexia come across words they cannot read they tend to either guess, skip the word or try to sound it out. Those strategies don't generally yield the results that the student needs to understand the word they struggling with. One simple strategy that helps the student focus on the word and its parts is to teach the student to spell the word out loud. For example, if a student comes to the word *actively* they should say: a c t ive ly. You should notice that they spelled each grapheme in the base separately and then the two suffixes are spelled together. It is this cadence that helps the students pay attention to the structure of the word. This often helps students eliminate the addition of letters that they tend to include when reading words they do not recognize and it stops them from guessing.

Morpheme wall

Another option is to have a morpheme wall. This is meant to be a living wall where new morphemes are added throughout the year as they are discovered.

Morphemes

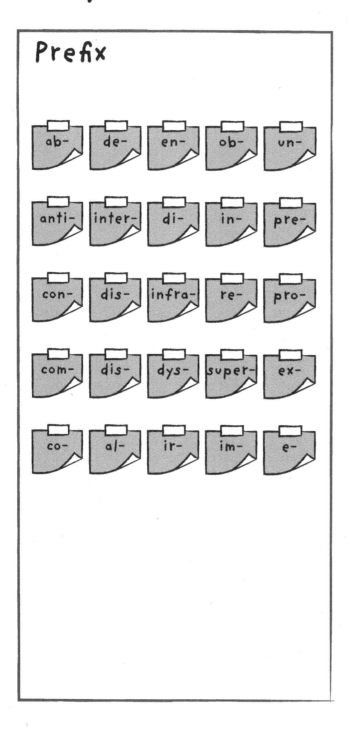

Prefix

ab- de- en- ob- un-

anti- inter- di- in- pre-

con- dis- infra- re- pro-

com- dis- dys- super- ex-

co- al- ir- im- e-

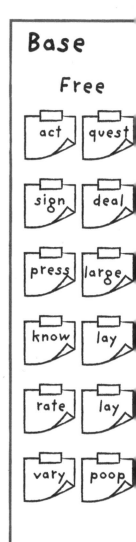

Base

Free

act quest

sign deal

press large

know lay

rate lay

vary poop

Connector vowels

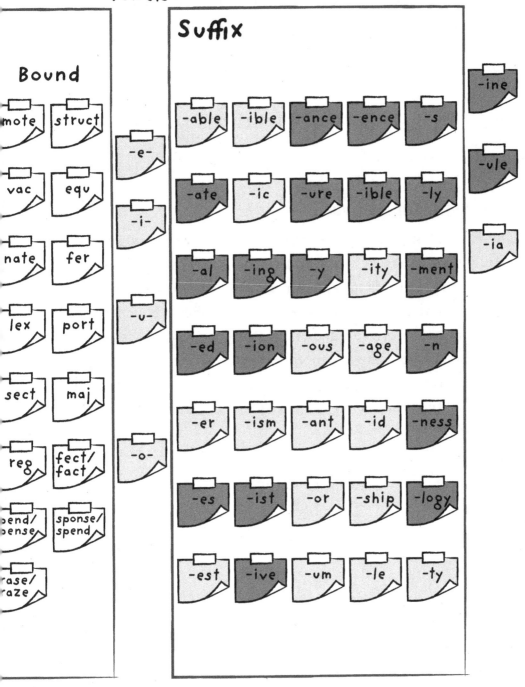

Bound

mote	struct
vac	equ
nate	fer
lex	port
sect	maj
reg	fect/fact
pend/pense	sponse/spend
rase/raze	

Connector vowels: -e-   -i-   -u-   -o-

Suffix

-able	-ible	-ance	-ence	-s
-ate	-ic	-ure	-ible	-ly
-al	-ing	-y	-ity	-ment
-ed	-ion	-ous	-age	-n
-er	-ism	-ant	-id	-ness
-es	-ist	-or	-ship	-logy
-est	-ive	-um	-le	-ty

-ine   -ule   -ia

Add a small, but important, qualifying word into your instruction

In the phoneme/grapheme walls example in the last chapter I included the sentence "<a> represents /a/ like in apple," but that sentence is very misleading. We can add one simple word to that sentence to help children understand our spelling system a little better. So, which word could have that much power? It is the word *can*. So, the sentence would change to "<a> *can* represent the phoneme /a/ like in apple."

Word sum manipulatives

One way to incorporate a multisensory component into the instruction is to create word sum cards. This is as simple as using different colored cards to represent different parts of the word sum: one color for the morphemes, one for the morpheme boundaries (+), one for the becomes arrow and one for the final word. In the example below, I chose to circle the morpheme boundaries (+) because my students often confuse them for extra letters in the word sum. That is a personal choice; you might find a different solution that works for your student.

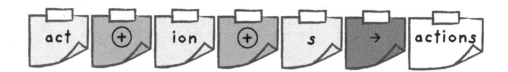

Tapping graphemes

For a word sum like play + ing → playing, have the student tap the graphemes of the base and the suffixes down their arm. For example:

p - l - ay -ing

The student taps once for each grapheme (p, l, ay) and once for each affix (ing).

Use Elkonin boxes

Elkonin (Joseph, 2000) boxes have been around a long time in the education world and they can be a great visual aid to help students understand the progression from phone to phoneme to grapheme.

	catch		
IPA symbols Phonetic Pronunciation	[k	æ	tʃ]
Phonemes Mental interpretation of the phone	/k	æ	tʃ/
Graphemes Letters or a group of letters that represent the phoneme	<c	a	tch>

Nonsense words and grammar

Spelling and grammar are interrelated and cannot be ignored when teaching spelling. Below are a few fun ways to incorporate grammar. Don't be afraid to try this with young kids too; remember, they understand that "I have two cat" is not grammatically correct, so they do intrinsically already understand grammar.

It is very common to use nonsense words to help students use what they know about the English writing system to practice using words they have not seen before. But those words are often out of context and that is not how English works. So, here is a fun, and more functional, way to incorporate nonsense words into your lesson. Below is the poem, Jabberwocky by Lewis Carroll.

'Twas brillig, and the slithy toves
Did gyre and gimble in the wabe:
All mimsy were the borogoves,
And the mome raths outgrabe.
"Beware the Jabberwock, my son!
The jaws that bite, the claws that catch!
Beware the Jubjub bird, and shun
The frumious Bandersnatch!"
He took his vorpal sword in hand;
Long time the manxome foe he sought—
So rested he by the Tumtum tree
And stood awhile in thought.
And, as in uffish thought he stood,
The Jabberwock, with eyes of flame,
Came whiffling through the tulgey wood,
And burbled as it came!
One, two! One, two! And through and through
The vorpal blade went snicker-snack!
He left it dead, and with its head
He went galumphing back.
"And hast thou slain the Jabberwock?
Come to my arms, my beamish boy!
O frabjous day! Callooh! Callay!"

He chortled in his joy.
'Twas brillig, and the slithy toves
Did gyre and gimble in the wabe:
All mimsy were the borogoves,
And the mome raths outgrabe.

Most of these words are nonsense words. Have the student study the words and then come up with some ideas about how the affixes change not only the form of the word but its grammatical function and explain how they came to that conclusion. You can step up the activity by asking the student to identify how these words function relative to other words in the poem. For example, for "frumious Bandersnatch" it can be hypothesized that *frumious* is an adjective based on the <-ous> suffix and it is modifying Bandersnatch, which must be a noun *in this context*.

For younger kids, you can easily find nonsense poems with a quick Google search, or, better yet, have students come up with nonsense poems and then identify the parts of speech based on the affixes they used to create the words. The key is the context. Spelling and grammar have to be studied in context in order to be understood.

Content area investigations

Students with dyslexia often struggle with content areas like math, science and history. Some of that struggle might be a result of not understanding the language being used. So studying the spelling of the words used in the content areas might help alleviate some that confusion. Below are examples of words that could be fruitful in understanding the language being used. I have included a matrix and word sums for the word *centimeter* and have listed some common words for the three content areas identified.

Centimeter

What does it mean?
One hundredth of a meter.

How is it built?

cent + i + meter → centimeter

This word has two bases, <cent> and <meter>. The second base could be <mete> and the affix <-er>; for now we will leave it as <meter>.

What are its relatives?
Century, centipede, cent, cents.

		meter/metre	
<cent>	i	pede	s
hundred	s		
	ure	y	es

What graphemes function coherently here?
The base <cent> can lead to a discussion about the different phonemes that <c> can represent and when the pronunciation shifts. In fact, that could be a descriptive generalization. There is an interesting phonology shift in this word family when the <t> in the base <cent> shifts from /t/ to /tʃ/ when the suffix <-ure> is added.

Content area discussion
Now the student can have a conversation about the fact that <cent> represents hundred just like there are 100 years in a century and a centipede has many legs.

Suggested content area words to study

Math: denominator, exponential, subtract, addition, decimal, centimeter, variable.

Science: biology, anthropology, electricity, variable, temperature, telescope, volume.

History: decade, president, civilization, constitution, democracy, millennium, revolution.

The point is that understanding spelling is not just about spelling; understanding spelling is understanding what the words mean and how those words are used in all different contexts. Talking about morphology and etymology should not be limited to the hour set aside for reading and spelling; it should permeate each topic.

■ CLOZE EXERCISE WITH WORD FAMILY

A cloze exercise requires the reader to fill in the blanks using the context of the sentences.

The _____ (family) thought the dog looked _____ (familiar)
     Noun   Adjective

You can create cloze sentences using topics you are currently studying. Additionally, you can create sentences that require words with the same base but different affixes, which can lead to a conversation about the effect the function of the word has on the spelling of the word.

We went to _____ (play) baseball.

He was the best _____ (player) on the team.

Henry hurt his hand while _____ (playing) tennis.

Commonly misspelled words

In an ideal world, understanding English spelling would be an organic process where the words that are studied come from conversations in the classroom. However, many people need a little boost to get started. One place to start is by investigating the most commonly misspelled words. Cramer and Cipielewski (1995) reviewed 18,599 written compositions of children in grades 1–8 (years 2–9) and noted spelling errors in these compositions. The results revealed that a small list of common words are misspelled the most. They complied a list of the 100 most frequently misspelled words across eight grade levels. These words are listed below and might be a good place for you to start your journey in helping students to understand the spellings.

too	didn't	like	about
a lot	people	whole	first
because	until	another	happened
there	with	believe	mom
their	different	I'm	especially
that's	outside	thought	school
they	we're	let's	getting
it's	through	before	started
when	upon	beautiful	was
favorite	probably	everything	which
went	don't	very	stopped
Christmas	sometimes	into	two
were	off	caught	dad
our	everybody	one	took
they're	heard	Easter	friend's

said	always	what	presents
know	I	there's	are
you're	something	little	morning
friends	would	doesn't	could
really	want	usually	around
finally	and	clothes	buy
where	Halloween	scared	maybe
again	house	everyone	family
then	once	have	pretty
friend	to	swimming	fired

■ SAMPLE LESSON PLAN

1. Previously investigated affix practice

Materials: Previously studied affixes written on square papers (i.e. 3x5 inch cards cut in half). Bases are also written on square paper sheets and placed on the table.

The student builds words using bases and affixes. The student identifies the affix, announces the spelling of the affix, identifies the base, announces the spelling of the base and then pronounces the word. The student must also use that word in a sentence to check that they know its meaning. This is also an opportunity to discuss pronunciation shifts in affixes like <re> and <de>, which can include a schwa.

- Suffixes: -ly, -un, -less, -ness, -ion, -s, -ed (all three pronunciations), -ing.

- Prefixes: re-, de-, un-, in-, im-, il-, ex.

2. Building words using previously investigated bound and free bases

Materials: Affixes and bases written on square papers (i.e. 3x5 inch cards cut in half).

Use the affixes from step 1 and two to three bases to create words. The student announces the word sum and then pronounces the word. The words have to be real words and words they know the meaning of. This can be checked by having them use the words in a sentence. Check for pronunciation shifts.

3. Choose a new word to study

Materials: Dictionary, blank matrix and lined paper.

1. Using the word investigation process outlined in this book, identify the base, relatives and pronunciation.

2. Write word sums.

3. Build a matrix.

4. Homework

- Choice 1: Write sentences using two or three of the investigated word sums.

- Choice 2: Using a list from the Word Searcher website (www.neilramsden.co.uk/spelling/searcher), which allows you to type in letter strings and then generates a list of words with that letter string, create word sums and place them in the matrix.

Next steps

Remember the word *antidisestablishmentarianism* from the preface? Do you have a hypothesis about the structure of this word? Do you notice any affixes? Do you know what it means?

My hypothesis is: anti + dis + e + st + able + ish + ment + are + ian + ism.

The base in this word is a bound base <st>, which means to stand.

This book is a starting place for you to discover how to share the information with your students. Be sure to check the resources section for suggested instructional aids and ongoing professional development. The blogs by teachers are especially useful, as they are written by teachers who are implementing this information and brilliantly share how they are doing it.

Take your time and try one activity at a time. Revel in your own discovering and your student's mistakes. Allow these discoveries and mistakes to be the guiding force in your lessons.

Glossary

Affix: An affix is a bound morpheme that is *fixed* onto the base or another affix (example: <act> + <ive> → active). Affixes include prefixes, suffixes and connecting vowels. Some examples of prefixes are: in-, de-, re- and mis-. Examples of suffixes are: -ing, -ed, -ion, -ive. Example: <re> + <act> + <ive>→ reactive. Suffixes can be further categorized into derivational and inflectional suffixes, which are listed in Chapter 3 as their own entries. The other type of affix is a "connecting vowel letter" as in the Greek <-o> connecting vowel letter in the word <morph + o + log + y> or the Latin <-u> connecting vowel letter in <act + u + al> or the <-i> connecting vowel letter in <face + i + al>.

Assimilated prefix: The word *illogical* contains the assimilated prefix of < il>. It is a variation of the prefix < in>. In Late Latin the prefix < in> assimilated to the following consonant, which in this case, was <l>. Despite the spelling changes of assimilated prefixes they maintain their meaning.

Examples: il-, im-, in-, op-, ad-, ap-

Examples: illogical, immature, innate, opposition, addition, application

Base: A base is the current spelling of an English word. Bases can be either bound or free. To identify a base as bound or free, you can start with a spelling, identify any prefixes and suffixes, then write a word sum. (See the "word sum" entry for a definition and an example.) In the word *replayed*, both <re> and <-ed> are identified as affixes. In this word sum, <play> has been identified as a *free base*, meaning it is a word on its own. Here is an example word sum for this free base:

$$replayed \rightarrow re + play + ed$$

In this next example, the base is identified as a *bound base*, which means it cannot stand on its own as a word and needs another morpheme to be a current English word. Here is an example word sum for this bound base:

$$unstructured \rightarrow un + struct + ure + ed$$

Connecting vowel: Connecting vowels are usually found in words of Latin and Greek origin. They often connect two bases but can connect suffixes, like in the word thermometer. The word sum for *thermometer* is therm + o + meter. We identify that <therm> is the base by identifying related words like *thermos* and *thermal*, which both share a meaning and a spelling. We identify <meter> as the second base by determining its meaning—to measure, and we have identified it as a free base (for the purposes of this example). Here is another example:

$$The <-o> in morph + o + loge + y \rightarrow morphology$$

Consonant: A consonant is a sound made with a closed or partially constricted vocal tract. For example, when you make the sound [f] the air is partially restricted by your teeth.

Content words: Content words carry specific meanings that can be defined. They are usually stressed within a sentence or clause. For example, in the sentence: "The cat is black," the words *cat* and *black* are the content words. They carry the meaning in the sentence.

Content words are spelled with at least three letters. The word *egg* has three letters because it is a content word, just like *inn*. Only content words follow the three-letter rule; there are no restrictions regarding the length of function words.

Decoding: Decoding is the ability to apply knowledge of phoneme/grapheme relationships to correctly pronounce/read written words. This does not include writing or comprehension.

Derivational suffix: Derivational suffixes are added to create new words. Derivational suffixes are added to a base, which results in another word, often of a different category (Ohio State University, 2016). Here are some examples:

act + ion → action

act + ive → active

act + ive + ly → actively

Digraph: Two letters that are used together to create a grapheme that represents one phoneme.

Encoding: Encoding is the ability to apply knowledge of phoneme/grapheme relationships to correctly spell written words.

Etymology: The study of the origin of words and how they have evolved through time. Most present-day English (PDE) words are the result of our evolution of language. English spellings are influenced by Latin, Old English, Greek, French, Old Norse and Dutch. For example, the word *ballet* originated in Late Latin *ballare* "to dance" from Greek *ballizein* "to dance, jump about," then it moved through Italian *ballette* and then Old French *balletto*, before becoming the English word *ballet*. Understanding the history and story of a word is an important component to understanding the current spelling of a word (Harper, 2001–2019).

Function words: The purpose of function words is to express grammatical relationships (SIL, 2018). Function words can be spelled with as many letters as necessary, but often take the shortest spelling that is acceptable. Here are some examples of function words:

the, in, of, because

Grapheme: A letter, or a group of letters, that represent a phoneme. In the word *chip* there are four letters: c, h, i, p and three graphemes: ch - i - p. In the word *chips*, there are five letters: c, h, i, p, s and four graphemes: ch - i - p - s and two morphemes: chip + s.

Homophones: Two or more words that share a pronunciation but have different meanings and/or spellings. Here are some examples of homophones:

two, to, too

see, sea

band, banned

Inflectional suffix: Inflectional suffixes can create different grammatical forms of words but don't change the meaning of the word (such as -s, -ed, -ing, -en, -ed, -er, -est). They are often located further from the base than derivational affixes and are often at the end of a word (SIL, 2018). Here are some examples:

run + **s** → run**s**

act + ive + ate + **ing** → activat**ing**

mean + **est** → mean**est**

International Phonetic Alphabet (IPA): This is a notation system that uses a set of symbols to represent each distinct sound that exists in human spoken language. The IPA notations are used to describe how a word is pronounced. This IPA chart contains the symbols for English. Here are some examples:

action using IPA is [ækʃən] /ækʃən/

shout using IPA is [ʃaʊt] /ʃaʊt/

Remember, the [ ] indicate the phonetic representation and the // represent the phonemic representation.

The IPA chart is below. The first provides the symbols for American English pronunciation. All of the symbols needed for all English dialects are provided but may be used differently. For example, the pronunciation of car in American English is /kɑr/ and the British pronunciation is /kɑː/.

IPA key for American English

Consonants		
Unvoiced	Voiced	Liquids
/p/ pan	/b/ ban	/ɔɹ/ for
/t/ to	/d/ do	/ɑɹ/ car
/k/cuts	/g/ guts	/ə/ mother (unstressed)
/f/ fan	/v/ van	/ɝ/ purple (stressed)
/θ/ think	/ð/ this, that	/ʊ/ fear, sheer
/s/ sip	/z/ zip	/ɛɹ/ bear, air
/ʃ/ shop	/ʒ/ vision	/l/ love
/ʧ/ chop, batch	/dʒ/ gym, badge	/ɹ/ room
/ks/ fox, Texas	/gz/ exactly	

Nasals	Other
/m/ **m**oney	/kw/ **qu**ick
/n/ **kn**ight	/h/ **h**appy
/ŋ/ so**ng**	/r/ litt**l**e, la**dd**er
Vowels	
/æ/ **a**t	/eɪ/ **ai**d
/ɛ/ **E**d	/i/ **ea**t
/ɪ/ **i**t	/ɑɪ/ tr**y**, m**igh**t
/ɑ/ **o**ff, f**a**ther	/oʊ/ **o**ver
/ʌ/ **u**gly (stressed)	/u/ m**oo**n
/ə/ **a**round (unstressed)	/ju/ **U**nited States
/ʊ/ b**oo**k	/ɔɪ/ b**oy**
	/aʊ/ c**ow**
Semi-vowels	
/w/ **w**in	/j/ **y**es, Kat**j**a

Source: Gail Venable and Rebecca Loveless

Lexical matrix: A matrix organizes a family of words, built from a base, which are related in meaning, spelling and etymology. They include the base, prefixes, suffixes and connecting vowels but do not have to be comprehensive. They are meant to be fluid and added to as students discover new words that belong in the matrix. A matrix has to be read from left to right and columns cannot be skipped. For example, to get to the word *displeasure*, the student will read the word sum as <dis> + <please> + <ure>. A prefix does not have to be included in each word, for example the word *pleasantly* does not include a prefix. The matrix below can be further developed to include other words with the <please> base. Matrices can be easily created with a blank piece of paper or for free online at: www.neilramsden.co.uk/spelling/searcher.

Prefix(es)	Base	Suffix(es)	
dis un	<please>	ant	ly
		ed	
		ing	
		ure	able

Morpheme: A minimal distinctive unit of a word that carries meaning and a sense of the word structure. This includes bases, prefixes, suffixes and connecting vowels. Here are some examples:

cat + s → cats (two morphemes)

play + ing → playing (two morphemes)

act + ive + ly → actively (three morphemes)

Morphology: Morphology is the study of the internal structure of a word, which is made up of morphemes. A morpheme is the smallest meaningful unit in a word. For example, the word plays is two morphemes: play + s → plays.

Morphophonemic: The English writing system is morphophonemic, which means that a word's morphemic structure will dictate how it is pronounced. For example, in the free base <please>, the <s> is pronounced [z]. When we add the suffix <-ure> the phonology of <s> shifts to [ʒ] and <ea> shifts from [i] to [ɛ]. The example provides evidence that it is difficult to know how to pronounce a word until we consider how the morphemes interact with each other.

Orthography: Orthography is the spelling system of a language.

Phoneme: A phoneme is the smallest unit of speech in a word that affects meaning. The phones [b] and [r] contrast in identical environments and are considered to be separate phonemes. The phonemes /b/ and /r/ serve to distinguish the word *bat* from the word *rat*.

Phonology: Phonology refers to the organization of speech sounds in a language.

Prefix: A bound morpheme that is fixed (pre + fix) before a base. Here are some examples:

dis- (dislike)

un- (unlucky)

mis- (misread)

re- (redo)

Root: The words *base* and *root* are often used interchangeably. In this book, the root is defined as the historical origin of the word. Words with a common root have the same etymological origin, but may not have the same base in PDE.

Semantics: The branch of linguistics and logic that studies meaning.

Stress: The schwa is what happens when we reduce or elide a vowel in the unstressed part of a word. Ladefoged and Johnson (2015) describe stress as something that "applies not to individual vowels and consonants, but to whole syllables. A stressed syllable is pronounced with a greater amount of energy than an unstressed syllable and is more prominent in the flow of speech" (p.259). English speakers often either reduce the vowels in unstressed syllables or omit the vowel completely. All vowels can be reduced and they can be reduced to more than just /ju/. For example, say this sentence in a normal conversational rhythm:

Our president was part of the family.

Now say this same sentence while pronouncing very clearly each and every syllable. This second rendition would be difficult for many native English speakers to understand. Most who have worked with struggling spellers have over-enunciated to help the student successfully spell words, but that isn't really helping the student because it is perpetuating the sound-it-out strategy and, outside of working with you, the speller will not encounter many people who over-enunciate.

Suffix: A bound morpheme fixed after a base. Here are some examples:

-ing (running)

-ion (action)

-able (comfortable)

-ly (lovely)

Syllable: A syllable is a unit of spoken speech. Syllables contain a nucleus, which is usually a vowel and can contain an onset and a coda.

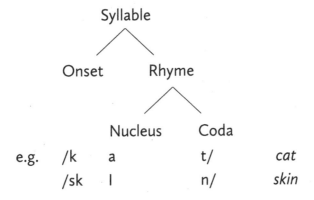

	Onset	Nucleus	Coda	
e.g.	/k	a	t/	cat
	/sk	I	n/	skin

Syntax: The arrangement of words and phrases to create sentences.

Word family: A set of words that share the same base. Word families are not the same as words that rhyme; those are rhyming families (think: *cat, bat, sat,* etc.). Here is an example of a word family:

please, pleasing, pleasure, pleasant, displeasure, unpleasant

Word sum: This is how those who study orthography reveal the underlying structure of words. Word sums combine morphemes from left to right and use the morphological boundary sign (+) to show a morpheme boundary (this can also be referred to as a join); → is the process arrow, which can be announced as "becomes." Here is an example of a word sum:

dis + rupt + ion → disruption

The word sum would be announced the following way (remember to spell the morphemes in the brackets < >:

<dis> **join** <rupt> **join** <ion> **becomes** dis rupt ion disruption

Vowel: A vowel sound is made when air through the vocal tract has limited obstacles and the vocal tract is open.

Resources

Your journey is not over; in fact, you have just begun. This is not your typical resources section. This book is just a drop of information in an ocean of understanding. In fact, this book could have been volumes long. You still have learning to do about Latin, Greek, French, Old English, IPA and etymology and this section guides you to resources to help you continue your learning. I encourage you to take some courses from the experts listed below. Take the time to read the mind-blowing blogs from teachers who are making this happen in their classrooms all over the world. Put your feet up and immerse yourself in the books listed; they will change your life. Most of all, enjoy the constant surprises that the English writing system reveals to us every time we study a word and watch your students come alive with excitement once they realize it's not crazy and they can make sense of it all.

Dyslexia books

Dyslexia Advocate! How to Advocate for a Child with Dyslexia within the Public Education System, by Kelli Sandman-Hurley

The Dyslexic Advantage: Unlocking the Hidden Potential of the Dyslexic Brain, by Drs. Brock and Fernette Eide

The Dyslexia Empowerment Plan: A Blueprint for Renewing Your Child's Confidence and Love of Learning, by Ben Foss

Essentials of Dyslexia Assessment and Intervention, by Nancy Mather and Barbara J. Wendling

Overcoming Dyslexia: A New and Complete Science-Based Program for Reading Problems at Any Level, by Sally Shaywitz

Proust and the Squid: The Story and Science of the Reading Brain, by Maryanne Wolf

Reading in the Brain: The New Science of How We Read, by Stanislaus Dehaene

Language at the Speed of Sight: How We Read, Why So Many Can't, and What Can Be Done About It, by Mark Seidenberg

Dyslexia websites

British Dyslexia Association: www.bdadyslexia.org.uk

Decoding Dyslexia, this website lists current advocacy efforts in American states: www.decodingdyslexia.net

Dyslexia Help: www.dyslexiahelp.umich.edu

Dyslexia Training Institute: www.dyslexiatraininginstitute.org

International Dyslexia Association: www.interdys.org

Learning Ally: www.learningally.org

Made by Dyslexia: www.madebydyslexia.org

TED Ed – What is Dyslexia?: www.youtube.com/watch?v=zafiGBrFkRM

The Yale Center for Dyslexia and Creativity: www.dyslexia.yale.edu

Understood: www.understood.org

Wrightslaw: www.wrightslaw.com

Books about the English language

The American Way of Spelling, Richard Venezky

A Course in Phonetics, Peter Ladefoged and Keith Johnson

The Stories of English, by David Crystal

Ongoing professional development websites

Dyslexia Training Institute, online courses about dyslexia, advocacy and Structured Word Inquiry, annual online conference: www.dyslexiatraininginstitute.org.

Wordworks Kingston, ongoing blogs posts, professional development in Structured Word Inquiry: www.wordworkskingston.com.

Real Spelling, ongoing spellinars that include the following topics: Latin for orthographers, Greek for orthograpers, transcribing Greek, Real Script and more: www.realspelling.fr.

See the Beauty in Dyslexia, provides online introductory Structured Word Inquiry courses: www.seethebeautyindyslexia.com/blog/transforming-a-resource-room-teacher.

Mrs. Steven's Classroom, online courses in grammar and Structured Word Inquiry: http://mbsteven.edublogs.org/grammar-class.

Blogs

Learning About Spelling, a blog about spelling: https://learningaboutspelling.com.

Mrs. Steven's Classroom Blog, by Mary Beth Steven, a blog from a group of students and their teacher: http://mbsteven.edublogs.org.

Smallhumansthinkbig, by Skot Caldwell (archived), a blog from a first grade (year 2) teacher: https://smallhumansthinkbig.wordpress.com/author/skotcaldwell.

Word Nerdery, by Ann Whiting, a blog about morphology and etymology: https://wordinquiry.wordpress.com.

Beyond the Word, by Lyn Anderson, a blog about investigating how the structure of the English spelling system really works: http://wordsinbogor.blogspot.com.

Mrs. Barnett's Buzzing Blog, by Lisa Barnett, a blog from a teacher about reading, spelling and writing: http://barnettsbuzzingblog.edublogs.org.

Rebecca Loveless, a blog from a Structured Word Inquiry coach: http://rebeccaloveless.com.

Instructional aids

Linguist-Educator Exchange, a website offering the following resources: Grapheme Deck, InSight Word Decks, InSights into Inflections, InSights into Auxillaries and Matrix Study Sheets: www.linguisteducatorexchange.com.

Wordworks Kingston, a teacher resource book, *Teaching How the Written Word Works*, offering an introduction to the core concepts of the ordered way that English spelling works. It uses a series of lessons designed to help teachers, tutors and parents make sense of English spelling along with their young co-learners. The lessons focus on morphological analysis with the matrix and word sum: www.wordworkskingston.com/WordWorks/WW_Revised_Teacher_Resource_Book_%26_70_Matrices_DVD.html.

Advantage Math Clinic, a website that has a deck of beautiful cards titled Truer Words, described as follows: "Each card in this deck explores a single, complete lexical item—a single written English word—as both a big-picture tapestry of a word family (front of each card), and through the Four Questions of Structured Word Inquiry (back of each card)": www.advantagemathclinic.com/truer-words-vol-1.

References

American Academy of Pediatrics, Section on Ophthalmology, Council on Children with Disabilities, American Academy of Ophthalmology, American Association for Pediatric Ophthalmology and Strabismus, American Association of Certified Orthoptists (2009) "Joint Statement—Learning Disabilities, Dyslexia, and Vision." *Pediatrics 124*, 2, 837–844. Accessed on 8 January 2019 at http://pediatrics.aappublications.org/content/pediatrics/124/2/837.full.pdf.

Apel, K., Diehm, D. and Apel, L. (2013) "Morphological Awareness Intervention with kindergartners and first and second-grade students from low socioeconomic status homes: A feasibility study." *Language, Speech and Hearing Services in Schools 44,* 161–173.

Aronoff, M., Berg, K. and Heyer, V. (2016) "Some implications of English spelling for morphological processing." *The Mental Lexicon 11*, 164–185.

Berko, J. (1958) "The Child's learning of English morphology." *WORD 14,* 2–3, 150–177.

Berninger, V. M., Abbott, R. D., Nagy, W. and Carlisle, J. (2010) "Growth in phonological, orthographic, and morphological awareness in grades 1 to 6." *Journal of Psycholinguistic Research 39*, 141–163.

Bowers, J. S. and Bowers, P. N. (2017) "Beyond phonics: The case for teaching children the logic of the english spelling system." *Educational Psychologist 2*, 124–141.

Bowers, P. N., Kirby, J. R. and Deacon, S. H. (2010) "Effects of morphological instruction on Vocabulary acquisition." *Reading and Writing: An Interdisciplinary Journal 23*, 5, 515–537.

Cramer, R. L. and Cipielewski, J. F. (1995) *Spelling Research and Information: An Overview of Current Research and Practices.* Glenview, IL: Scott, Foresman and Company.

Carlisle, J. F. (2010) "Effects of instruction in morphological awareness on literacy achievement: An integrative review." *Reading Research Quarterly* 45, 464–487.

Devonshire, V., Morris, P. and Fluck, M. (2013) "Spelling and reading development: The effect of teaching children multiple levels of representation in their orthography." *Learning and Instruction 25*, 85–94.

Diliberto, J., Beattie, J., Flowers, C. and Algozzine, R. (2009) "Effects of teaching syllable skills instruction on reading achievement in struggling middle school readers." *Literacy Research and Instruction 48*, 1, 14–28.

Ehri, L. (2000) "Learning to read and learning to spell: Two sides of a coin." *Topics in Language Disorders 20*, 19–36.

Goodwin, A. P. and Ahn., S. (2010) "A meta-analysis of morphological interventions: Effects on literacy achievement of children with literacy difficulties." *Annals of Dyslexia 60*, 183–208.

Gottardo, A., Chiappe, P., Siegel, L. S. and Stanovich, K. E. (1999) "Patterns of word and nonword processing in skilled and less-skilled readers." *Reading and Writing: An Interdisciplinary Journal 11*, 5–6, 465-487.

Joseph, L. M. (2000) "Using word boxes as a large group phonics approach in a first grade classroom." *Reading Horizons 41*, 2, 117–127.

Harper, D. (2001–2019) *Online Etymology Dictionary*. Accessed on 8 January 2019 at www.etymonline.com.

IDA (2011) *Spelling*. Accessed on 28 January 2019 at https://dyslexiaida.org/spelling.

IDA (2019) *Definition of Dyslexia*. Accessed on 28 January 2019 at https://dyslexiaida.org/definition-of-dyslexia.

Kemp, N., Mitchell, P. and Bryant, P. (2017) "Simple morphological spelling rules and not always used: Individual differences in children and adults." *Applied Psycholinguistics 38*, 1071–1094.

Kirby, J. R., Deacon, S. H., Bowers, P. N., Izenberg, L., Wade-Wooley, L. and Parrila, R. (2011) "Morphological awareness and reading ability." *Reading and Writing: An Interdisciplinary Journal 25*, 389–410.

Ladefoged, P. and Johnson, K. (2015) *A Course in Phonetics*. Stamford, CT: Cengage Learning.

Leong, C. K. (2000) "Rapid processing of based and derived forms of words and grades 4, 5, and 6 children's spelling." *Reading and Writing: An Interdisciplinary Journal 12*, 277–302.

Moats, L. (2005/6) "How spelling supports reading: And why it is more regular and predictable than you may think." *American Educator (Winter)*.

Nagy, W., Anderson, R. C., Schommer, M., Scott, J. A., and Stallman, A. C. (1989) "Morphological families and word recognition." *Reading Research Quarterly 24*, 262.

Nunes, T., Bryant, P. and Bindman, M. (1997) "Morphological spelling strategies: Developmental stages and processes." *Developmental Psychology 33*, 637–649.

Ohio State University (2016) *Language Files: Materials for an Introduction to Language and Linguistics, 12th Edition*. Columbus, OH: Ohio State University.

Sandman-Hurley, K. (2016) *Dyslexia Advocate! How to Advocate for a Child with Dyslexia within the Public Education System*. London: Jessica Kingsley Publishers.

SIL (2018) SIL website. Accessed on 28 January 2019 at www.sil.org.

Torgesen, J.K., Wagner, R.K. and Rashotte, C.A. (2012) *TOWRE-2 Test of Word Reading Efficiency—Second Edition*. Austin, TX: Pro-Ed.

Venezky, R. L. (1967) "English orthography: Its graphical structure and its relation to sound." *Reading Research Quarterly 2*, 3, 75–105.

Wagner, R. K., Torgesen, J. K., Rashotte, C. A. and Pearson, N. A. (2013) *CTOPP-2: Comprehensive Test of Phonological Processing, 2nd Edition*. Austin, TX: PRO-ED.

Index

by the same author

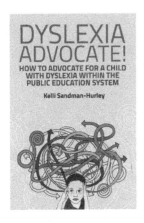

Dyslexia Advocate!
How to Advocate for a Child with Dyslexia
within the Public Education System
Kelli Sandman-Hurley

Paperback: £14.99 / £22.95
ISBN: 978 1 84905 737 0
eISBN: 978 1 78450 274 4
200 pages

This straightforward guide provides the essential information for parents and advocates to understand US law and get the right educational entitlements for a child with dyslexia.

Using case studies and examples, this book demonstrates clearly how to apply the Individuals with Disabilities Education Act (IDEA) to the unique requirements of a dyslexic child. It offers simple, intelligible help for parents on how to coordinate successfully with their child's school and achieve the right services and support for their dyslexic child; up to and beyond getting an effective Individual Education Plan (IEP).

Dyslexia Advocate! is an invaluable tool for parents trying to negotiate a complex legal system in order to get the best outcome for their child. It is an essential guide for anyone who is considering acting as an advocate for a child with dyslexia.